How *to* Attract
MEN
and *Money*

How *to* Attract
MEN
and Money

How to Marry the Right Man
and Help Your Husband Make a Fortune

Rosa Lee Hill & Napoleon Hill

Published and Distributed by
SOUND WISDOM
PO Box 310
Shippensburg, PA 17257-0310
717-530-2122
info@soundwisdom.com
www.soundwisdom.com

While efforts have been made to verify information contained in this publication, neither the author nor the publisher assumes any responsibility for errors, inaccuracies, or omissions. While this publication is chock-full of useful, practical information, it is not intended to be legal or accounting advice. All readers are advised to seek competent lawyers and accountants to follow laws and regulations that may apply to specific situations. The reader of this publication assumes responsibility for the use of the information. The author and publisher assume no responsibility or liability whatsoever on the behalf of the reader of this publication.

The scanning, uploading and distribution of this publication via the Internet or via any other means without the permission of the publisher is illegal and punishable by law. Please purchase only authorized editions and do not participate in or encourage piracy of copyrightable materials.

Text design by Susan Ramundo

ISBN 13: 978-1-64095-313-0
ISBN 13 eBook: 978-1-64095-314-7

For Worldwide Distribution, Printed in the U.S.A.
1 2 3 4 5 6 / 25 24 23 22 21

*Blessed is the man who has come to know
that our muted thoughts are our sweetest thoughts.*

*Blessed is the man who from the blackest depths can see
the luminous figure of love and seeing, sing; and singing say:*

"Sweeter far than uttered lays are the thoughts I have of you."

Contents

Introduction

By the Napoleon Hill Foundation

This book, written in 1940, may be enjoyed on two levels. First, it offers an historical view of what the roles of a successful husband and wife were as the Depression in America was coming to an end. Napoleon and Rosa Lee were newly married, successful in business, wealthy, happy, and optimistic, and all this comes through in this book. Second, it contains timeless advice on how to attain success, happiness and personal achievement. Written by Napoleon Hill and his wife Rosa Lee Hill just three years after the publication of the classic *Think and Grow Rich*, the book reflects the research, experience and insights of Napoleon and the understanding, perception and wisdom of Rosa Lee. The lessons taught here apply not just to marriage but to all aspects of life.

This edition differs from the first edition only in the respect that some material was deleted because it was deemed by the Foundation to be unduly repetitious of material in Napoleon Hill's previous books. However, nothing was added to the book, or revised. Every word in these chapters appears as it was written by the authors.

Please enjoy the new foreword to the book by J.B. Hill, Napoleon's grandson, which follows this introduction, and get ready to be entertained and educated.

–Don Green
Executive Director, Napoleon Hill Foundation

Foreword

The Story of Rosa Lee Hill
by J. B. Hill

Rosa Lee Beeland was born on December 16, 1905, in Harriman, Tennessee, the daughter of William H. Beeland from Alabama. Her mother died just three weeks after her birth. Since her father worked for the railroad, she was raised by her mother's sister. Rosa Lee was a delightful child with exceptional beauty. When she was three years old, she won a contest as the most beautiful child in Atlanta. By 1930, she was working as a secretary in advertising and had completed two years of business school.

When Rosa Lee was 28, she met Napoleon Hill in Alabama, where he was lecturing. According to a *New York Times* article, Rosa Lee was a woman of "dazzling beauty and steamy sex appeal." Although Napoleon was nearly 53 at the time, he looked 20 years younger and had the health and vitality to match his dynamic speaker's image. The two fell madly in love, were married, and settled into a small apartment in the Hell's Kitchen area of New York City. Napoleon's son Blair and his new wife Vera Cunningham also lived with them while Napoleon wrote *Think and Grow Rich*.

According to Blair, Napoleon dictated the manuscript to Rosa Lee, who typed and later edited the manuscript. They worked night and day on the book, neither needing more than four hours of sleep. In 1938, the money started rolling in, and Rosa Lee moved with Napoleon to

Florida. Rosa Lee dwelled in the limelight of affluent society for a while, co-authored *How to Attract Men and Money* with Napoleon, and then filed for divorce in 1941, obtaining the copyrights to all of Napoleon Hill's works in the settlement. She then quickly married Cecil Houston Lichliter. (The Hill family oral tradition, perhaps unfounded, is that Cecil was Rosa Lee's divorce lawyer.) This marriage also failed, as Rosa Lee Beeland was single again in 1943 when she joined the Women's Auxiliary Corps during World War II as an aviation cadet and earned a commission as a lieutenant.

During 1944, she served on recruiting duty in California, where newspaper accounts record that she recruited "a show girl" of some note. Throughout the remainder of the war she served on General MacArthur's staff. During the 1950s, Rosa Lee worked as chief associate editor for *Popular Mechanic's Magazine*, and in the late 1960s she served with the Peace Corps in Micronesia.

Rosa Lee moved to Ormond Beach, Orange County, Florida, in 1969, where she worked as the Director of Social Affairs at the Ormond Hotel. She was still single when she died in 1970 at the age of 65.

How to Attract Men and Money was written at a time when a good marriage was every girl's dream and finding the right man for marriage was the ambition of every girl. Rosa Lee may not have believed it was right to marry for money, but she certainly did not mind marrying where the money was. Her book explains how a girl from the 1940s should do exactly that. The book is a whimsical look back at a time when women were women and men were men. I am not sure how society survived.

–J. B. Hill

From the 1940 Edition

Publisher's Preface

Do dreams ever come true? Does it ever happen in real life that a Cinderella finally does meet her Prince Charming, marry him, live in a Castle—and continue happily ever afterward? Can a woman, early in life, build her ideas of the kind of a man she wants to marry, and the things she wants—and through planning, belief and faith—eventually make Life pay on her own terms?

And if such an achievement (which would seem to be the secret hope and aim of most every woman) can be definitely and deliberately brought to pass—by just what means is it done? Surely, there must be millions of single women, and as many more who are married, who will ask this question and be keenly interested in the answer.

Well, Rosa Lee Hill, wife of America's number one Success-philosopher, has accomplished these laudable aims, and she has written this book to tell women just how she did it. It teaches the actual Philosophy she has followed.

And now at the age of 35, she has all the blessings any woman could ask of Life. She has personal charm; therefore, she has a right to tell other women how to acquire it. She has the man of her choice; therefore, she is capable of telling other women how to attract the men they want. She is engaged in work she loves and from which she gets abundant happiness; therefore, she can counsel other women on how to acquire it.

Here is a woman who refused to marry until she was almost 30 because she knew the type of man she wanted and was determined to accept no other. When she found him, he was at the bottom of the ladder of a great national misfortune that had changed the lives of millions of strong men.

He hadn't a dollar left, but she married him, blended her mind and heart with his—through a peculiar, little-understood, and never-taught (until now) art of Sex-Transmutation. Now, between them they have acquired in a few short years both material and spiritual values sufficient to enable them to share with others the most important part of their fortune.

Get the secret, explained in this book, by which Rosa Lee helped her husband to stage a comeback, and you will have the pass-key to whatever you demand of life, whether it be a mate in marriage, money, happiness, or something else. She has proved her discovery to be sound by making it bring her a beautiful Castle for a home, freedom for the work she loves to do, and has brought to her a famous husband with whom she is perfectly happy at all times.

To the skeptical who may believe she "married money," it can be confessed that they started married life a few years ago in Hell's Kitchen (one of the most desolate parts of New York City), where Napoleon Hill had been left when the tides of depression finished with his fortune. So, they started "at scratch." The money, and all the material possessions they now own and enjoy, came solely as the result of the philosophy described in this book.

Best results from the following lessons will be experienced by married people, and those contemplating marriage, if they will read it together and discuss it frankly as they read. It has enough sound counsel to straighten out the most disagreeable family snarl. It contains enough practical advice to enable any husband to stage a comeback after having been defeated in his occupation or business.

It very plainly suggests practical tests by which an unmarried woman may choose a husband intelligently, with more than average assurance that she can help him make good in life. The author of this book writes on these intimate and important subjects from her own experience—and the reader should remember she is making Life pay on her own terms.

Some members of the author's own sex may severely criticize this frank confession of the secrets with which she attracted and married the man of her choice. But most of them who read the book to scoff will remain to pray at her shrine, for truly it has been written out of the fullness of a grateful heart so that other women could share her riches.

We cannot imagine either unmarried or married people to whom the pages of *How to Attract Men and Money* will not bring a new understanding, a new courage and hope, a new power, and a new happiness.

—The Publishers

Introduction

The Author's Personal Experience in Winning
and Holding the Right Man

Because I sincerely wish to share with every woman the secret through which I have found happiness and accumulated riches of a priceless nature, I shall make this intimate personal confession:

When I was a very young girl, long before I entered high school, I knew I would marry a distinguished man. I am married to him!

My mother died when I was born, and I went to live with an aunt who taught me to call her "mama." One day, my father heard me call her mama, took me on his lap and explained to me that my mother was dead, and I should call my aunt by her correct name. Torn between two fires, I went outside and began to cry. My father came out, discovered why I was crying, then took me on his lap again and said something which governed my entire life: "Hereafter," said he, "you call your aunt whatever you wish, and always remember you cannot please everybody, so try to please yourself."

From that day until this, I have tried to live naturally by pleasing myself. I have been rewarded by more of the blessings of life than most women ever enjoy, but no one should jump at the conclusion that I have been blessed without effort on my part. My blessings are of my own creation, otherwise I would have no right to publish this book advising other women how to get what they want. Moreover, I have never trampled upon the rights of others.

I live in a beautiful mansion, located in Florida, on a high rolling hill of many acres covered by beautiful trees, overlooking a gorgeous lake which gives us miles of unobstructed vision.

Here, my husband and I maintain what we believe to be the most unique home in all the world. We are adopting and rearing 15 boys and girls. We are proving, through these children, that there is nothing wrong with the younger generation except their parents, some of their teachers, and many adults whom they are trying to ape.

Our family is not yet complete, but we have gone far enough with our experiment to feel confident we can send our children back to the world from which we took them, fully prepared to encounter and master all the evils of the day, and to master all chances of economic distress.

Outside of our home, our wards are submitted to all the usual inharmonies among people; inside our home, they never feel the influence of a negative thought, much less a negative word.

Each child is taught the truth that both happiness and misery begin as a state of mind, and that a state of mind can be controlled and made to order; nay, that this is the only thing any human being can control completely.

If you had reached the conclusion that I am a selfish woman thinking only of her own joys and pleasures, you must now, in fairness to yourself, reverse your opinion. I do believe I am the happiest woman living, and I can sincerely say I desire to share my happiness with all who are willing to pay the price to receive it. That is the major reason why I am writing this book.

This world is no longer a man's world exclusively!

Surely it has been proven that a woman can take her place alongside of men and make life yield happiness, in competition with the keenest of male minds, if only she will learn to condition and control her own mind. Happiness is not an elusive thing, available to only the few.

I am happy every minute of the day because I have followed certain definite rules for acquiring and holding happiness. These rules are described fully in this book, but I wish to emphasize that my greatest insurance against unhappiness is my habit of helping others to find it in abundance.

This world is no longer a man's world exclusively!

My major justification for writing this book is to share my riches with other women who have not yet found the road to happiness. Inasmuch as the most precious thing I possess consists of my relationship with my husband, I have no alternative but to explain how I found him.

Perhaps my frankness will seem less mercenary if I explain that my career as the wife of a philosopher whose books are best sellers, precludes all possibility of my being a private citizen. Of necessity, a large portion of my time and my life belong to my husband's friends and followers; therefore, I shall deliberately pull aside the curtains that shield us from the public view and give the best description possible of our home.

Some may criticize me for frankness in analyzing the more intimate side of my private life, but how else could I share the philosophy that has helped me to force from Life complete happiness?

Some will not like the title of this book, on the grounds that it, too, suggests a mercenary philosophy, and I am sure the title will cause many people to ask, "What of the author? Has she attracted her man, and all the money she wants, or is she some disappointed old maid who is seeking an opportunity to satisfy her hungry soul by writing a preachment to other women?"

It is but natural that most people would want to know the answer to these questions; therefore, I have answered frankly, and I hope satisfactorily.

To begin with, let us ask and answer another question. Why does every woman want a man and plenty of money? There can be but one answer. Women want men and money as a means of finding happiness. The only place one can find love-in-a-cottage—unless it is a pretentious cottage—is in the lines of the poets. Poverty and happiness do not make congenial bedfellows.

Because of this knowledge, every woman is seeking a man, unless she has already found him, and enough money to give her the material things of life. Of course, some women are seeking not merely a man, but *the* man; the one and only man who can bring into their lives the mental, physical, and financial equivalents of happiness. Other women seek only a man, any man who can supply a meal ticket, while some demand luxury.

In this book, I have presented a complete practical philosophy, consisting of the factors through which women may attract both desirable men and money. The reason I know the philosophy is practical, that it will work, is the fact that it has worked perfectly for me.

I have found the man—perhaps the only man through whom I could have acquired happiness in its highest form. Through my association with my husband, I have not only found happiness, but all the money

I need and more. By the application of the philosophy described in the pages you are about to read, I have not only attained the highest goal for which any woman can aspire—complete happiness—but my husband has attained the same goal.

When you come to the chapter on the Spirit of Romance, you will know that my riches consist not just of material wealth. I have found love and romance in the particular form which thrills the heart of any woman. You will know, as you read this chapter, that it was written straight from the heart, and I want you to know that I have known, and continue to know the spirit of romance only because I have lived by the principles set forth in this philosophy. This bit of personal confession may seem intimate and direct, but I want every reader to get my viewpoint before reading the book.

I began planning to attract my man—the right man—when I was 15 years of age. My planning gave no little concern to my relatives because it took on the nature of unorthodox behavior in that I permitted no match-making on the part of interested relatives and friends.

For some reason which I cannot explain, I was fortunate enough to realize, even at the tender age of 15, that there was something more to be sought in marriage than a meal ticket, and the privilege of bearing children. From the very outset, I made up my mind that before I would marry any man, he would have to prove to me that he had ambition above mediocrity, that he had ability to rise above the commonplace, that he had a mind as well as a body, and that he would make intelligent use of his mind.

I had seen all I wanted to see of "hoof-and-hand" men, men who are merely willing to go through life earning an existence with the aid of their feet and hands. What I wanted, and what I was determined to find, was a man who had a mind and knew how to use it.

The years went by rapidly. I had almost reached the age of thirty before the ideal which I had built in my own mind came to claim me—but he did come, and he was the exact man I had created in my own mind. His coming, our meeting, and our marriage all were so dramatic that I must tell you the story. I tell it only because of the direct bearing it has on the philosophy outlined in this book.

As strange as it may seem, when I was building my dream man in my "sophisticate" fifteen-year-old mind, my husband was building in his mind a dream woman. The picture fitted me perfectly, even down to the color of the hair, the educational background, and a score of other smaller details. So, when the great cosmic forces of Nature brought us together, we recognized each other quickly.

As most of the readers of this book already know, Napoleon Hill is a philosopher and author. Acting upon his own philosophy, he decided, several years ago on the first of January, to find his dream woman within six months. On the same day I reached the conclusion that I would find my dream man within the same length of time. I call particular attention to these two facts because they are important; we both knew what we wanted, but this was the first time in our lives that either of us actually got around to setting a definite time for acquiring it.

As a means of carrying out his intentions, Mr. Hill went into the South on a lecture tour. At Knoxville, Tennessee, he was given a banquet by his students on his last night in that city. The banquet was a surprise affair. At the close, he was called upon to make a speech, so he arose, looked around for a moment or two, then suddenly announced that he was going to take his students into his confidence and tell them of his greatest aim in life. He then launched into a description of his dream girl, and finished by saying, "I do not know her name, or where she lives, but I do know that she has been in my heart for 15 years, and I shall find her very soon."

At that very moment, his manager was on the way to Birmingham to make arrangements for Mr. Hill's next lecture. For some reason which never was explained, his manager switched plans and went to Atlanta instead. When the change was brought to Mr. Hill's attention, he was not at all pleased, but there was nothing left for him to do but go to Atlanta.

When his class opened in Atlanta, it consisted of about 100 very charming women of all ages, temperaments, and personalities, and of course, many of them were looked upon by Mr. Hill as "suspects," a few as "prospects," for his dream woman. I shall never forget what happened when I was first introduced to the man who was to become my husband. He looked me over with a sweep of his eye which went from my head to my feet and back again, then bowed and walked quickly away. I learned later that he scratched me from his "suspect" list at the first glance, because he thought I had "too much good looks and too little brains."

I followed him into the auditorium, listened to his lecture, and before he had finished I recognized him as being the man for whom I had been waiting all those years. Moreover, I made up my mind that I would marry him. Of his background, I knew nothing. Of the difficulties I might encounter in order to marry him, I knew nothing, but I did know that Napoleon Hill would be my husband.

Was I in love with him? No, I was not in love with him, but I was in love with his mind, with his hopes and ambitions, with his achievements. He was physically attractive and all that, but his mind was the force that really attracted me.

There was something about the tone of his voice, the fire of his enthusiasm, the expression on his face, which clearly telegraphed to me the knowledge that I was sitting in the presence of my future husband, yet I had met him just a few moments ago.

After the lecture was over, I made known my discovery to my friend who had introduced us. She smiled knowingly and said, "Wait and see what happens."

When the class instruction was completed, the students were invited to see Mr. Hill privately about their personal problems. I was the last to be interviewed. Never will I forget what happened that afternoon. A business-like secretary formally announced me and seated me at a considerable distance from my future husband. The interview proceeded along very prosaic lines for about fifteen minutes, then his face suddenly turned as white as a sheet. He began to fidget around like someone who was ill. He got up and pranced around the room, went back and sat down in a seat somewhat nearer me. He got up again, pranced around some more, then sat down again. His mind was obviously not upon the question of finding and solving my personal problems. Finally, he arose and announced the interview was to be postponed until the following afternoon. He escorted me to the elevator and very formally dismissed me.

I went immediately to call on my friend and we held an indignation meeting. "If he saw no more in you than his actions indicated," she snapped, "then he is a fake and I wouldn't give the snap of my fingers for any solution of personal problems he would offer."

The joke was on both of us! What he had actually seen in me was his future wife, the "dream woman" he had been building for 15 years. He had made the discovery at a most embarrassing moment, in the midst of a professional interview in which he dared not digress from professional ethics by expressing personal feelings.

The next afternoon, I went back to complete my interview. I did not share my friend's feeling of pessimism. When I arrived, he met me at the elevator, escorted me to his study, and without inviting me to be seated, started immediately to tell me his story. We talked for more than five hours. We compared notes, and spoke very plainly and frankly. There was no sham on either side. There was no attempt on the part of either of us to appear to best advantage.

Before I left, we were engaged. Then we were married.

My people were shocked beyond words. The very idea of marrying a man whom the family had not met! The very idea of passing up men of whom the family approved, and marrying a man on a mere hunch was more—much more than they could understand. But I understood it, I still understand it.

I found the man of my choice through the great universal law of Harmonious Attraction. I first created him in my own heart and mind. I nurtured and kept him alive with the spirit of my own hopes and aspirations. When he came, I knew him because I had seen him, in my own mind for 15 years.

We have been married long enough to have had our first misunderstanding—but we have not had it. We shall never have it because we are perfectly attuned to each other. Love did not enter into our marriage at first. We both agreed that we had enough in common, outside of love, to bring us happiness and congeniality. About three days after our marriage, I began to fall violently in love with him. A few days after, he began to fall as violently in love with me. We are now inseparable, and the basis of it all is the strict application of the philosophy I am presenting in this book.

I attracted my husband through the application of the principles I have here recommended, and I have held him through the same principles.

Between us, we are not only finding and enjoying happiness in its highest form, but we are rendering useful service to thousands of others who are seeking the goal we have attained.

Our first joint work, in which we injected the influence of the "Master Mind" created by the harmonious alliance of our two minds, was a book entitled, *Think and Grow Rich*. That book has had a strange influence on those who read it. The influence is strange to others, but not to us. We know of what this influence consists. We know what has been injected into the lines of the book, and back of the lines, which has caused so many of its readers to take a new lease on life. We know that the book is inspiring its readers to really think for themselves, because the book was not written at all—it was lived by its authors.

So this is my answer to the question, "What of the author? Has she attracted her man and all the money she wants?"

If I am correct in my assumption that women want men and money so they may find happiness, then I have attained the goal for which every woman is, or should be, aiming for, for I have found complete happiness. As to my material wealth, it seems almost sacrilege to mention material things in the same breath that one acknowledges the possession in great abundance of the highest form of spiritual blessings, but I have all the material wealth I need, and more.

As a part of my wealth, I have acquired something other than the man and money, which I value greatly; I have gotten rid of the habit of being eternally bound by habits.

My husband and I work when we are in the mood for work, which is almost 12 hours out of every 24. We sleep when we are sleepy, get up when we are rested; we eat when we are hungry. If company comes to call, we receive without formality, in whatever clothes we happen to be wearing, generally suited to comfort. We have no family secrets. The mail is placed on the office table in the morning and it is read aloud by one of us. All important decisions are reached jointly, by analysis and discussion.

The experiences of life are varied and often imponderable, therefore no one can be expected to explain the causes of all that happens throughout a lifetime. I cannot help wondering why so many marriages go on the rocks, why so many men and women are miserable in marriage, why so few women find the right man and the money they desire, when the way to this desirable end seems clear and so easily followed.

When you begin the search for the right man, remember that he may be the one to whom you are now married, despite the fact that you may have found neither money nor happiness. Remember that men can be changed, and of all the forces on earth best in position to change them, none equals woman.

This book was written to encourage women to try for whatever they want from life, and not be satisfied with whatever Life hands them.

Before it was written or could be written, I had to demonstrate the soundness of the philosophy it conveys. That is why I felt privileged to begin the book with this very frank statement of what the philosophy has done for me. If some feel that my confession savors of vanity or over-frankness in connection with the more intimate side of my life, my only reply is that I feel the good that may be accomplished by thus giving hope and courage to other women, more than offsets the offense.

Remember that men can be changed, and of all the forces on earth best in position to change them, none equals woman.

Despite all the evils of which people all over the world are complaining, I believe this to be a grand world because I have so related myself to it that it gives me what I want. I live in a world that belongs to me because I created it in my own mind.

My world is so completely filled with pleasant thoughts and useful deeds that I have no time to be unhappy, and the beauty of it all is the fact that I have found romance in everything and everyone that influences my life.

I am happy to have been privileged to demonstrate that a woman may maintain a happy and successful marriage and at the same time follow a career of her own choosing which in no way interferes with her marriage. I believe my husband would say that I have made for him exactly the sort of home he desires, but I have not stopped there. I have gone a step further and so related myself to his work that I am of continuous help to him.

I edit all his writings and serve as a buffer between him and people who try to appropriate his time unnecessarily. Moreover, I lend him my own mind as a sounding board for every idea he expresses, and

I think he would tell you that I am neither his woman Friday nor his "yes" woman. Frankness and directness between us at all times is our number one rule for keeping out of personal controversies. If I ever got to the point where I had to feed my husband's ego by agreeing with him just to please him, my greatest usefulness to him would be at an end.

I mention all these details only to show that a successful marriage is not a matter of accident or coincidence. I know well enough that most women who meet with disappointment in their search for the right man and the material riches of life fail because they do not put into their own part of the bargain, that which it takes to ensure happiness.

It is one thing to want the right man and plenty of money, but it is something else to find these blessings and hold them!

Happiness is something that can be kept only by giving it away! Without happiness, there can be no permanent romance. Without happiness, love sneaks out at the back door and disappears. Without happiness, money is only so much inert matter. Some people believe they could be happy if they had plenty of money. Do not be misled. It is not true. Happiness can be transmuted into money, but money by itself cannot be transmuted into happiness.

Through my husband's literary works—his magazine and newspaper articles—we are reaching thousands of men and women who are searching hither and yon for happiness. Every one of these to whom we bring even the slightest degree of happiness contributes, through the immutable law of Compensation, to our own store of life's blessings.

This is why Life to us is just one continuous experience of romance. We find romance in everything we touch. We find romance because we are looking for it, expect and demand it, and refuse to accept any substitutes for it. Our relationship with our children abounds with romance. We find romance in our relationship to our secretariat and our household staff because we are in harmony with all these. We believe it both important and significant that every member of our household shares liberally in the atmosphere of romance we have created in our home; so much so, in fact, that members of our secretariat are constantly being offered positions at more money than we pay them, and our housekeeper has but recently attracted and married the man of her choice.

Romance and worry do not make good bedfellows; therefore, we refuse to give worry any portion of our thoughts. This is easily managed because there are only two sorts of worry—one connected with the things we can control, and one connected with the things we cannot control. We spend no time worrying over the things we cannot control; instead, we use the time to better advantage in directing the things we can control.

Romance is a state of mind; therefore, it is but a portion of the one and only thing in all the world any human being can control; his own mind!

My husband and I enjoy romance in its fullest measure because we are related to each other, and to every other person with whom we are closely associated, in a spirit of friendliness, sympathy, understanding and harmony. We make no demands of one another other than that for perfect harmony.

Romance is a state of mind.

We find, too, that both harmony and romance are the natural outgrowth of our habits. Habits are contagious! That is why every member of our household and every friend who has the privilege of visiting freely in our home and many of the casual visitors find it so very difficult to indulge in worry while they are within range of our influence. It explains, also, why thousands of readers of my husband's books write letters from all parts of the country describing with boundless enthusiasm this "something" that greeted them from every page and gave them courage for a new start after having met with some form of adversity.

These are intimate expressions of thought, but I am happy to share them with every reader of this book because I can sincerely say they describe, as well as one could do so through the printed pages of a book, an intangible power which is the very warp and woof of the riches with which Life has so abundantly blessed me. That power, expressed in simple language, is nothing more nor less than a state of mind known as the right "mental attitude."

Only through the appropriate "mental attitude" can any woman attract and hold the love of any man. That is why I have stressed the importance of romance, as romance is nothing but "mental attitude."

PART ONE

Preparing to Attract

CHAPTER 1

The Spirit of Romance

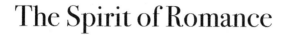

*M*any people associate romance with the days of knights in armor, of ladies in distress in some high tower, of fanciful and fantastic exaggerations of the era of King Arthur.

But is there no romance today? If there were no romance, how would you and I be able to exist in such a hustle-bustle as goes on about us every day?

True, when I was living in the midst of seven million people on Manhattan Island, all rushing about constantly, I could find no southern moonlit evening sweetly scented with magnolias peeping out from the wax-like leaves. I could find no Spanish moss dripping from the trees; I could hear no mocking birds singing in the moonlight; but I could remember the many times I had been in these places; I could even make them live again if I chose.

The reason we often believe these romantic surroundings essential to the spirit of romance is because they are conducive to dreaming, planning, constructive and positive thinking, and living the dreams we have suppressed. But, the truth is, we must romance before we can love. We need not always fall in love with some tall, dark, and handsome Prince Charming—no! We may fall in love with life itself, with our work, with the career of a man who is far from handsome—but—until we romance, dream, plan, and actually see the dew upon the rose of Life, we are without the spirit of romance.

You may say that you do not wish to become sentimental and mushy. Are sentimentality and mushiness even akin to romance? I believe the difference between sentimentality and romance is this: sentimentality is living with the past; romance is living with the future. There is a vast difference. The past is forever gone, the future is forever approaching. It is pliable in the hands of one who knows what she wants, and has faith in her ability to shape it.

Sentimentality is living with the past; romance is living with the future.

Unfortunate, beyond estimate, is the woman in whose heart the luminous torchlight of romance has been permitted to die; for that woman must kindle anew this God-given force of personal charm or be deprived forever of her greatest source of attraction.

Circumstances connected with one's obligations to others may sometimes result in suppression of the spirit of romance, but there never can be adequate justification for any form of neglect of this beautiful emotion which permits it to wither and atrophy through disuse. There is always the possibility of transmutation of the emotion of romance into some work of art, some form of constructive service that will keep it eternally burning.

Until you are able to romance, to dream, to plan, and have faith in your dreams, you are entirely without that magnetic charm which is the quality that makes an otherwise prosaic and uninteresting woman into a fascinating woman who stands out from the crowd.

If it is true that a woman may "make" or "break" a man, it is true because of woman's mystic power in the spirit of romance with which she may lift a man high, or drive him down to the depths of despair.

Women who have suffered disappointment because of some circumstance of unrequited love should know that the fragments of a broken romance may be assembled into some form of creative effort, some work of art, some thing of beauty that will compensate for any disappointments, no matter how great.

The oak sleeps within the acorn, and the bird waits within the egg, no more surely than the seed of creative ability and charm sleep within the heart and brain of every normal woman in whom lives and moves this great irrepressible spirit of romance. Each of these and every impulse that lies dormant in one's mind must gain expression through some form of outside stimuli.

The acorn yields an oak tree only through the stimulus of the sun's rays. The bird breaks the shell and takes to the wing only in response to the warmth outside itself. The seed of charm germinates and takes on some form of action in response to emotions, the greatest of which are love and sex blended into the spirit of romance.

There is a tendency today to neglect, or even discourage, the romantic side of life. Perhaps this is the very reason there are so many broken homes, so many miserable marriages, and so few really great loves. Certainly romance never paved the road to any divorce court. Certainly no woman ever lost her husband because she had the spirit of romance; no husband ever lost his wife because he had the spirit of romance. When the spirit of romance exists in a home, there can be no bickering, no scrapping, no hatred, for hatred and bitterness cannot bloom in the garden of romance.

On woman hinges the success or failure of the home. On woman rests the development and advancement of mankind. Upon woman rests the responsibility of the enlightenment of the world. These are great responsibilities, and we must take the burden of our share, and do the best we can to carry our little contribution of development and advancement to the world, through ourselves, our husbands, and particularly through the development of our children.

It is woman who has been taught through centuries of abuse, ignorance, and persecution the art of patience and tolerance and understanding. In the few years of freedom that women have had (chiefly in this country), the strides she has made are almost unbelievable. The knowledge that she has gained is due to thousands of years of thirst for knowledge. The plans for constructive development that she has begun are the outgrowth of centuries during which she was treated as a chattel.

All this has come through the romancing of woman, through quiet, deeply rooted longing, planning, dreaming of the day when she would have a place in the world, when she could really build and construct; for woman—the real spirit of womanhood—is essentially constructive. If man has developed into a destructive beast when given power, it is because he is without the guidance, love, and encouragement of a woman who possesses the spirit of romance. All down the ages, every great man has had behind him the spirit of an understanding woman.

Perhaps the most outstanding example is the immortal Lincoln. Though Ann Rutledge did not love him with the same deep love she gave a less worthy man, she was his inspiration, his idol. The loss of Ann Rutledge was the crossroad of Lincoln's life, and, but for the spirit of that wonderful woman, he would always have been but another country lawyer.

It was not Lincoln who sat in the White House and gave human kindness and understanding to a nation in chaos. It was the spirit, the confidence, the fairness of Ann Rutledge that made Lincoln immortal. It was the spirit of Ann Rutledge that caused his image to be carved in marble in a memorial at our nation's capital. When we go to stand at the feet of America's son, we pay homage to the man, but we pay silent tribute to the power of woman.

Napoleon was made a great man by Josephine, and though he was egotistical, grasping, and domineering, in the hands of Josephine he was putty. It was to be great in her eyes that he made himself the Emperor of France. Once he became too interested in himself aside from glorification for her eyes, he crashed with miserable disgrace.

Go back as far as you like in history, and though the woman may be unsung, unknown, you will find behind every great man, from Lincoln to the most modern immortal, Edison, a woman who built him to greatness. She built her man with the spirit of romance. She romanced with him, dreamed, planned the career, the greatness to which she aspired for her man.

In this, mothers particularly have a definite hold on men. Nature has chosen to grant woman the privilege of bearing the future generation, thereby influencing it from the moment of conception to the age of understanding. In this, woman has her greatest opportunity to build men of strong character, constructive thought, and to make her son worthy of a niche in the hall of fame.

These are inescapable facts. They cry out in a voice that echoes far down the ages, to the beginning of civilization. They are facts which have left their footprints on the Sands of Time.

Wherever evidence of greatness is found, whether in man or woman, there one may find the spirit of romance. Crush this great spirit and goes with it the creative forces of human beings.

Whosoever besmirches the emotion of romance thereby publishes to the whole world ignorance of one of God's great enduring gifts through which civilization has been refined.

Those who look upon this Divine source of creative effort with scorn bind themselves eternally with the bonds of mediocrity. Those who squander this blessing through sensuality and lust, or permit it to die of neglect, brand themselves as ignorant. The woman who belittles the spirit of romance in her husband thereby writes herself an insurance policy against all possibility of his economic success, and more than likely she will live to collect on that policy.

Subdue the spirit of romance in your child and thereby consign it eternally to the wearisome treadmill of misery and toil.

Ignore the call of romance, and thereby brand yourself as one who has lost hope. Listen to this messenger when it knocks at the door of your heart, treat it with civility and understanding when it arrives, and it will hand you the key to Life whose doors open only through your heart and brain.

They who treat lightly the spirit of romance confess to their ignorance of the attributes of personal charm.

Ah! You would love to romance—but it is too foreign to your surroundings, it is too intangible, too elusive? How can you rekindle this old fire which has been smoldering so long within you? Will it help to attempt to fan the flame? What good will it do? And how can you go about it?

These are questions which many women are asking themselves, and which should certainly be answered, but the spirit of romance is the one quality which makes dull work no longer dull; which makes monotonous days fly with the swiftness of joy, pleasure, and the beauty of the spring, even in this modern world.

To the woman who would say that romance is dead, let her draw nigh and give ear to the wondrous winged words that speed from lip to ear when youth meets youth and finds life sweet. Let her see the remarkable change that possesses men and women who come under the magic spell of love. Let her dream again the dreams that live alone in the hearts of those fired by the tenderest passion to possess the world. All that is great and good in man and woman comes to be there only through the godlike gift of love. Only when men are touched and moved by the Ennobling Flame that burns away the dross and leaves their spirit sweet and pure and strong do men see:

> "The face that launch'd a thousand ships
> And burnt the topless towers of Ilium."

'Tis then that the ennobled spirit of romance whispers: "Sweet Helen, make me immortal with a kiss."

I cannot say just what would be the most effective way for you to build and to keep alive the spirit of romance, but for ourselves, my husband and I have devised a little plan which keeps us always reminded of the beautiful side of life. We keep six roses always on our living room table. These six roses have certain meanings. They stand for Love and Romance; Faith and Hope; Peace of Mind and Prosperity.

We began dreaming of these things long before we were entitled to all six of the roses, but we kept them there; and now, we actually possess all six of the things for which they stand.

We call them our little Entities, our little Friends who have helped us through the thin spots, who have kept our hearts in the stars when things were blackest. We see that they are always there.

By this activity, the very fact that we must attend to this little duty ourselves (we never leave our little Entities to anyone else), we are reminded every morning of the six most important things in our lives. By changing the water, we notice if one has drooped, or if one fades before the others, we wonder which of the six little Entities has been abused, and by whom. We check upon ourselves. It is surprising just what this will do.

Flowers are beautiful within themselves, but flowers with a definite purpose often speak more loudly than words, scoldings, or praises. The regularity of the action put into the upkeep of the tribute to our little Entities keeps us reminded of the things we must guard and protect.

These may not be the things which will suit you, but it would be a good plan to map out the things you want most in the world, the things for which you can be thankful. Then set them up as your entities; see that the proper number of flowers are kept on the shrine. This will serve as a constant reminder to yourself, and to those about you—particularly your husband, or prospective husband.

Every woman should seek the six entities which we use, for these six qualities, when blended into one state of mind, give one a certain indescribable lure or power of attraction not procurable in any other way. Make these six positive entities your closest neighbors and very soon they will help you to empty your mind of every care and every negative thought and every source of annoyance. They will take you gently into the land of peaceful slumber each night, and they will awaken you with the spirit of joy and gratitude in your heart the next morning.

Form a speaking acquaintance with these unseen friends, and never again will you find it necessary to go to sleep at night without a heart buoyed by a feeling of hope for what tomorrow will bring. After all, the greatest thing in life is not that which lies in the past, not that which has been buried in the deep chasm of one's subconscious mind; nor is it any material thing one now has. The greatest thing in life is a state of mind, the hope of future achievement! Something one expects, something as yet unattained! Contemplation is always sweeter than realization! The truly great psychologists are agreed on this.

I have said so much about the mind and its importance in your personality that you may believe there is little else; certainly there is nothing else as important, for the mind governs everything else within you from the very depths of your heart to the smile or the frown on your face. This may as well be accepted, for you can find no psychologist who will for a moment deny it. It is the ruling factor in your personality. And, granting that you have a positive, constructive mind, with malice toward none, it is essential to a charming personality that you color your mind and heart with a bit of beauty; and that beauty is essentially the touch of the aesthetic loveliness of romance.

We individuals go through personal "depressions" from time to time, during which we lose material things which we covet and prize highly, apparently without rhyme or reason, but there is a reason for our loss! It begins to manifest itself the moment we permit hope and faith to wither. Any person who goes to bed at night without taking inventory of tomorrow's blessings; or any person who, when taking inventory, sees only discouragement and despair for the morrow is on the threshold of a personal "depression."

Remember the pioneers of the world in all callings were men and women with keenly developed spirits of romance. Men and women who could and did dream of realities before creating them. There is something closely akin between the dreamers of the world and those gifted with the spirit of adventure and romance.

This new and changed world that came into existence because of the economic collapse will require men and women dreamers gifted with the spirit of romance and adventure to put their dreams into action. The dreamers have always been the patternmakers of civilization, and dreamers are romanticists who build a make-believe world into factual reality.

We boast of the accomplishments of our forefathers in the days when this country was a wilderness. We feel proud of their stamina in sticking to hardships and fighting against great odds to lay the foundations of this country. But we are quick to say those days are gone— those opportunities are forever behind us.

But how many of us are willing to take upon our own shoulders the burdens which this modern world has created? We can only see that our beautiful clothes are worn out, and no money to buy more. We can only grumble when we must dismiss the maid and do the work ourselves. We can only complain when we must pitch in and do the hard tasks which depression and necessity have conspired to bring upon us.

There could be no romance in this commercial world. There could be no room for building dreams and hopes when the whole world is in a state of chaos. Tell me when the world has not been in a state of chaos?

I know two women very well, and when you compare them, you will be able to decide for yourself if it is worthwhile to inject the spirit of romance into the very prosaic business of living.

The first woman used to have a great deal of money. She had an ample income and security. Life was a matter of entertaining herself, and it rocked along with the nicety of boredom until the "powers that be" swallowed the security which produced the income. She took it on the chin, put her shoulder to the wheel, and began the task of "filling in" with producing income until such time as the security would be reinstated.

Time went by. Conditions grew worse. It finally became evident that she was no longer working on a temporary basis, but it had settled down to the point where her income was needed—and was expected. It would always be expected, for her husband had no desire to work hard enough to produce enough for the whole family.

With a sigh, she accepted her fate. No complaint. No nagging, but her whole attitude changed to one of resignation. She accepted her fate and acknowledged that she would continue bearing her cross without so much as mentioning it to others. There she is, and in that rut she will remain—a woman to be pitied and respected. A woman leading a broken life in the grim silence of the condemned.

The second of these women used to have money, too. She had security and ample income. And similar conditions caused these to be removed. What did she do? She sat down with her husband, together they discussed what to do. Should she go into business and try to help make money, or should she stand by him while he made a come-back? The decision was reached. She would take upon her shoulders the responsibility of rebuilding a home.

They took a part of their meager savings and bought the cheapest virgin land which they could find. He set up a shop, plying his trade in a most humble fashion. Together they cleared the land.

Once this heaviest of work was done, the woman took upon her own shoulders the work of a man. She did carpentry work, painting, hard labor—actually pumping water from an old-fashioned pump, cooking on an old-fashioned stove, using kerosene lamps (try that someday, and see how you like it). She contributed everything she had, not only in physical labor, but she began to make of the little log cabin a show-place. It was a far cry from that when she began to plan for it. She put the spark of life in her husband, in her neighbors, and in friends. She lived every moment of every day for she was building her future, literally laying a board at a time to the home which would someday be a show-place.

This Christmas, she is having her first big party. All her friends for miles around are invited to come and share with her the beauties of her home—the greatest of which is her shining personality and the unbelievable spirit of romance which was used as the hammer to drive each nail, the brush to paint each stroke, the spade to dig the bed for every flower, as well as the magnet to draw close to her every person who comes within range of her unbelievable charm, which she has created out of the spirit of romance.

A fishing boat may be an exceedingly unsightly and very smelly thing, but when the waters are glistening with the sparkle of phosphorescent reflection of the moon, and the sails of the little boat are black against the silver of the night, the clumsiness of the boat, the fishiness of it all are lost in the exquisite beauty of the moment. And so, with woman, if she would remove herself from the ordinary, she should first beautify her mind and bathe it in the love, the beauty, and the warmth of the spirit of romance.

When I speak of romance I have reference to the habit of finding the interesting and helpful portions of every human relationship; not merely to the exchange of emotional feelings between men and women. My husband and I follow the habit of dramatizing the important facts of life in such a manner that we can easily appropriate them to our own use. This habit places in our hands the initiative in every situation affecting our happiness, and largely accounts for our privilege of saying that we are riding Life instead of being ridden by it.

This habit of transmuting important facts into practical romance has brought us usable knowledge which grew out of experiences that would otherwise have been of little benefit to us. The habit enabled us to reach definite conclusions on 15 important subjects, each of which we have under our control, viz:

1. We have learned the necessity of closing behind us the doors leading to all experiences of a negative, unpleasant nature. Moreover, our policy on this subject is so final that we not only close doors between ourselves and the things we do not want, but we lock them so tightly they never can be opened. We have particularly closed and locked the door between ourselves and all manner of fear, the habit of finding fault with each other, procrastination, worry, greed for material things beyond the amount of ordinary needs, the habit of accepting from Life substitutes

for that which we desire and demand, controversies with any member of our family or household, and most important of all, any situation or circumstance which has the slightest possibility of disturbing the relationship of perfect harmony and sympathy of purpose existing between us. Against all these things the door has been so closely locked that no power available to human beings can open it.

2. We have learned that every adversity and every form of defeat carries with it the seed of an equivalent benefit, therefore we never accept any such condition without searching until we find and appropriate the good it brings. This policy, alone, is sufficient to keep alive the spirit of romance.

3. We have learned that all people are where they are and what they are solely because of their own "mental attitude" toward themselves and others; that mental attitude is the attracting force which brings opulence and plenty, or the repelling force which permits poverty and misery to become the master. So we have formed the habit of keeping our mental attitude attuned at all times to correspond with the exact things we demand of Life. Romance and a negative mental attitude simply cannot occupy the same mind at the same time.

Romance and a negative mental attitude simply cannot occupy the same mind at the same time.

4. Our observation of men and women who are eternally in difficulty with one another, and always miserable and poverty-stricken, has impressed us with the fact that a bad disposition is the forerunner of everything that disturbs human relationships; therefore, we make it a part of our established policy to keep ourselves mentally and physically flexible by maintaining

good dispositions. Our own experience has proved that both good and bad dispositions are the outgrowth of definitely controllable habits.

5. Having learned that no one is ever entirely ready to begin anything, we have adopted and religiously follow the habit of starting right where we stand, and of working with whatever tools and materials we have available, when we desire to accomplish a given goal. We began this habit by marrying before the circumstances were entirely as we would have liked for them to be, and we have kept it up on every occasion which brought us face to face with the necessity of reaching a decision.

6. Our "mental attitude" having been kept under control and at all times positive has taught us that all habits, good or bad, become automatic through repetition, as the result of the law of Hypnotic Rhythm, the sum and substance of which is this: Nature forces environmental influences upon every living thing, and man is but the sum total of the daily habits he voluntarily establishes or those he acquires through indifference, all of which are set to a definite rhythm, by Nature, and are thereby automatically given irresistible momentum. To harness and use this law beneficially, one has only to establish any desired habit and to repeat it (by force if necessary) until it is picked up and taken over automatically by the law. In this manner does Nature adjust every living thing, (from the most tiny seed of vegetation to the most intelligent human being) to conform perfectly to the environmental influences in which it exists. Thus it is easily understood why the most important habit anyone can form is that of voluntarily maintaining a mental attitude favorable to the building and procuring of that which one demands of Life, for it is mental attitude which makes one's habits positive or negative.

7. Having learned that Life will yield the things one wants just as graciously as she will hand over the things one does not want—providing one has a definite policy of never accepting substitutes—my husband and I remain adamant when once we have established our goal and never make concessions or accept any form of defeat or discouragement as being more than a needed urge to greater resolution and sterner action.

8. Having been taught from practical experience the difference between being FOR something and AGAINST something, we have so budgeted our time and have so established our mental and physical habits and our mental attitude, that we are FOR many things and AGAINST but few. We devote most of our time to developing and extending the objectives in which we are interested, in promoting the things that bring us happiness and other forms of riches, which automatically consumes our time and leaves no room in our lives for any form of destructive effort. We leave to others the job of tearing down, annihilating, and destroying, and we admit of course that there are influences in the world which need to be suppressed and destroyed.

9. Believing that the person who moves on the side of initiative has a tremendous advantage over all who move only when pushed, we follow a definite habit of knowing what we want and of going after it without delay. We follow the same rule in deciding what we do not want, and in closing the door against it tightly.

10. Having agreed that poverty is a sin to all who accept it as a necessary condition, we will no more tolerate even the thought of it than we would permit our food to be poisoned. We believe that both poverty and riches begin in the form of "mental attitude";

that poverty results when mental attitude is not voluntarily made to order and controlled.

11. Knowing that Life consists of many things one can control and some that one cannot control, we have adopted a well-defined policy of relating ourselves to the things we cannot control in the best possible manner to insure us against damage, while we accept full responsibility for wresting from the things we can control whatever we demand of Life. We never substitute alibis for desirable achievement in connection with the things we can control.

12. We have learned the futility of depending upon others for that which we ask of Life, having discovered that an ounce of self-reliance is worth a million tons of dependence. Our habit of helping ourselves before expecting or asking help of others has had the effect of providing us with voluntary and willing cooperation from both other people and the imponderable forces of natural law.

> *An ounce of self-reliance is worth a million tons of dependence.*

13. Having learned that THINKING is the process of correlating, organizing and using FACTS, we never permit ourselves to indulge in or give expression to opinions not formulated upon what we believe to be facts. This saves much valuable time we might otherwise dissipate in trying to solve the problems of the world, or to help other people live their lives our way. Our policy saves us, also, from the necessity of accepting and depending upon the opinions of other people when we have reason to believe their opinions are based more upon their desires than they are upon facts.

14. Having discovered that one's closest associates have a definite tendency to influence both menial attitude and daily habits, we will not tolerate close association with any person who disturbs the harmony we maintain in all our professional, personal, and social relationships.

15. Knowing of the benefits of relaxation, meditation and play, we have developed habits that enable us to empty our minds of all serious thoughts, at will, as we have learned that practical thinking is not possible when the mind is strained and tense.

We have not only conditioned our own minds through the strict observance of the 15 principles here mentioned, but we have so related ourselves to our children and the other members of our professional staff and our household that they, too, receive great benefits by collaboration with us.

In these 15 points, you have a brief description of our conception of a practical application of the spirit of romance, for there is no escaping the fact that our daily habits consist in the main of a very definite use of these principles. When you reach my husband's analysis of our marriage and professional relationship in a subsequent chapter, you will profit by remembering that our success has been due directly to strict application of these 15 principles.

This is my answer to the person who complains that she has no time for romance. It is my answer to the person who looks upon romance as being nothing more than an emotional relationship between men and women. Through my description of the 15 principles, I have outlined the major influences which give my husband and me the privilege of saying we want nothing from Life which we do not already possess.

Romance is the charm of female character;
without it no woman can be interesting.
It is that poetry of sentiment which imparts to
character or incident something of the beautiful
or sublime; which elevates us to a higher
sphere; which gives an ardor to affection,
and a life to thought, and a glow to imagination.

PART TWO

Developing the Personal Qualities That Attract Men and Money

CHAPTER 2

Let's Consider Ourselves

*T*here are only two things essential to the happy, complete, and well-rounded life of the average woman: the right man and plenty of money. With these two assets, any woman can get everything else her heart desires to make her life entirely complete.

Some women leave it up to luck, chance, or Fate to find the right man, money, and happiness. The odds are too great to take this hazard. Perhaps you may have one chance in a hundred million of getting such happiness, for Life does not offer the best packages in the grab-bag or on the bargain counter. Life extracts full price for her gems. For those who are willing to pay the price, to lay the plans, and who know exactly what they want, Life gives great rewards.

Women cannot go out with a gun and hunt the right man as a hunter in the field. She cannot buy him with money. She cannot conquer him in battle—not the right man. There is but one way she can get him: She must attract her man, and before any woman can attract men, she must first make herself attractive!

Once a woman has attracted her man—provided she has selected the right one—she and he together can attract money, success, and fame of untold extent. This, of course, is meant for the woman who demands of Life complete happiness. There are some women who ask nothing of happiness, but only money—money at any price. Some women marry for it, others go into business to get it, still others devise rather shady schemes for obtaining it. Money has a strong lure, but it is a heartless companion, a fickle and faithless friend, when it is all one has.

Frankly, every woman should sit down with herself and decide just exactly what she wants in life, just what she demands, and lay a plan for obtaining it. Life is a cruel master when it has the upper hand, but once you take control, it is a most humble and gracious servant.

Every woman has the right to happiness, to master Life, and to attract to her the things she wants. But how does she do this? Through what power does she attract the things she wants in Life? The power through which woman attracts things has been given many different names. Sometimes we call it "personality," sometimes "charm," but always it is that certain something which is made up of a beautiful mind, a clean and unselfish heart. These things can be developed deliberately. We can actually grow into personalities of charm and magnetism, and should spend our time and energy developing the real qualities that go to make charm, rather than squander our time with mere veneer and polish, for the veneer will chip off and display its shallowness at the most crucial moment, and we are exposed as mere shams.

The easiest and most definite way in which to develop and cultivate charm is by a positive development of fifteen qualities which are vital contributing factors to the thing we call charm and personality; plus one other thing—a fair understanding and adjustment to present-day conditions and sociological problems. These 15 qualities are:

1. A Positive mind

2. The ability to face facts

3. A Definite plan of work

4. Poise

5. Sincerity of purpose

6. Harmony

7. Good sportsmanship

8. Courtesy

9. Conversation

10. A pleasing voice

11. Showmanship

12. Personal appearance

13. Good health

14. A normal sex life

15. The spirit of romance

Nature, in her wisdom, gave mankind control over but one thing in all the world—his own mind. This does not mean that man has made the best use of this power, nor does it mean that he uses it at all, for in too many instances, he does not; but every human being has the right to absolute control over his own mind.

Mind-control is an entirely separate and distinct thing from self-control. Mind-control is the power to give your mind the thoughts you wish it to feed upon, and to keep out of your mind all thoughts which you do not wish to lodge there. Self-control is the control over your actions or words, when you have lost control of your mind. For instance, when you display a temper, you do not have mind-control or self-control; but when you feel your temper rise, and refrain from displaying it and saying the ugly things you are thinking, you are displaying self-control but not mind-control, for you are allowing negative thoughts to lodge in your mind. Temper is not a part of the person who has complete control over her own mind.

Perhaps the most effective way in which to begin to develop mind-control is by setting a definite program of self-discipline. This must be mental discipline as well as habit discipline through the development of the qualities described in the following chapters. The first step in mental discipline is the actual facing of facts and conditions as they exist, not as we sometimes try to think they exist. It prohibits a blind ignoring of circumstances and facts, and denies you the pleasure of kidding yourself.

But, you ask, would life be worthwhile if I had to keep such a tight hold on myself, and live with such rigid discipline? What would it be worth? It would be complete freedom from worry, real self-confidence, real poise, high ambition, animation, and a keen interest and love of life. It would mean that you could actually demand of Life the best She has to offer and get it, for the woman who has control over her own mind, and knows what she wants, always puts into action a plan that brings her everything she demands.

Many women will say, "But I do know what I want." I can frankly say that, in many instances, this is not true. It is astonishing how few people can answer the question, "What do you want more than anything else in the world?" In fact, can you answer it? Unless the question can be answered instantly, without hesitation, and with absolute definiteness, you do not know what you want!

There must always be a first choice, and subordinated to that, and dependent upon it, other things may be desired and accomplished. But the first choice must be very definite. You must recognize just what it is and stick with your aim until you have achieved your goal.

If it is a husband that you want, is it "just a husband?" How any woman could want anything in the world above the love and companionship of some one man who belongs to her is more than I can understand. Notice, please, I say the love and companionship—not just a husband. There is such a difference!

If love is placed at the top of the list, then everything else must be subordinated to that one desire, until it is actually a reality. If there is a desire for money, which is secondary, this may be accomplished after you have found the right man—provided you take into consideration the things which you are looking for in your man.

There are some men who dream big dreams, think big thoughts, act big deeds, and make big money. There are other men who fit into the medium scale of life; they are good providers in a secure but small way, colorless, and more even of disposition and temperament than the flashing man of big ideas. Then there is the type of man who is just once removed from the poor farm all his life. He is the shiftless, ne'er-do-well who makes his woman's life a miserable lot.

It is well to consider just what you want—love or money—or both. Be sure before you lay your plans, for if you think it's money, minus love, you may find yourself a poor little rich girl with no one to love. If you think it's love in a cottage—or love in a shack—you may find the days long and the washboard a drab and back-breaking occupation; you may wish for pretty clothes, fine cars, and lovely diamonds.

It is probably more important than anything else in life to know just exactly what you want, for somehow the people who do know exactly what they want find ways and means of getting it.

You may say this is well and good for the woman who has not married and cluttered up her life with people who are standing in her way. But, is this necessarily an insurmountable obstacle? There is one thing which I cannot emphasize too strongly in the discussion of knowing just exactly what you want: the frank facing of facts. When you find you have made a mistake and are involved with people who are not in harmony with you, it is always best to sit down with yourself when you can be alone for a whole afternoon or evening, where there will be no noises or disturbances. Take with you a pencil and piece of paper. Sit for a few minutes quietly with your eyes closed. Relax your hands in your lap, and make your mind a total blank. This will relax you, and give you a fresh start with your task.

When you have relaxed for a few minutes, take the pencil and write down the one thing you want most in all the world. In this you must be very definite and specific; you must not deal in generalities.

Next, ask the question, "Will it hurt or damage anyone if I attain my desire?" If it will hurt or damage anyone, then the answer to this question, "Am I willing to bear the burden of responsibility for the hurt or damage I shall do?" remains between you and your conscience. This is something you must decide for yourself before you can go further.

Granting that your desire will injure no one, you then should list on paper every obstacle standing in your way. This done, begin to lay plans for surmounting each obstacle, one by one. This will set your mind to work on constructive, positive plans which will eventually lead you out of the jungle and to the goal you are seeking. I do not mean that merely writing a few words on paper can help you. It is the actual facing of circumstances as they exist, the recognizing of every obstacle, and definite planning of ways and means of surmounting each hindrance that will count. This is the method by which one builds a positive, constructive mind, and develops mental discipline. This is the method of thinking which builds a positive personality that radiates charm and happiness. This is the method of thinking which can enable every woman to attract to her the things she wants in life.

There are those who claim it is easy enough for the young and beautiful to do the things in life that they wish, and to have the things they desire, but they say that when one has passed the early twenties or the thirties, it is pretty hopeless. Hopeless? How mistaken they are! This is the one big error of the people who try to describe personality. Personality and charm are entirely removed and separated from youth, looks, race, or nationality. Personality and charm come from the inside of a person, actually radiate from within the very heart of the individual.

This was most dramatically proved to me in the personality of one of my best friends. This individual is a woman—not young and beautiful—but one who has passed the years we term as the most profitable years. Nevertheless, she is a woman who is making the best of what she has, and that is very much more than most women are doing. This woman is without doubt the most attractive and charming woman of my acquaintance, and at the same time the most perfect example of just what personality can do for one when properly developed. She is proof that age, beauty, and money are entirely unrelated to personality and charm. This is an exceedingly strong statement, but it is true—oh! how true!

Let's take a look at this lady, who at the age of 75 inspires such a sweeping statement. Note the age, please; 75, for there are few readers of this book who are quite that far along the road. Yet Esperanza Garrigue is decidedly the youngest person of my acquaintance, for she has the busiest, the most youthful mind of anyone I know. She is constantly planning, working; yes, she works for a living, and is independent.

She lives in the very heart of the artistic circles, teaching young hopefuls the art of singing. And, though she is an excellent teacher, I have no doubt the philosophy and sound counsel she gives helps them to keep up the fight all through life. I was at a musical she gave one evening and it was astonishing to study how definitely her personality dominated the entire group. Every person there had come, not so much to hear the voices (though they were lovely), as to bask in the sunlight and charm of Mme. Garrigue.

As she met each individual at the door, her big brown eyes flashed and sparkled, each person felt he or she was the guest of honor. Somehow she conveyed that feeling of warmth with every word and gesture.

Then the programme began. It moved smoothly for a while, but as always happens, Madame, in "straightening up for the occasion," had tucked one particular piece of music under a couch. No doubt you have found yourself in such a predicament many times—I know I have—and the natural thing to do is "just skip over that one," and not allow the guests to think for a moment that such a thing could possibly happen to you.

But not Madame! No. She remembered where it had been tucked, got down on all fours, pulled it out, and the programme proceeded as planned. Nor was she rattled, embarrassed, or apologetic; she was perfectly human about it, and no doubt every person there felt as I did, that above everything else Mme. Garrigue was human and not entirely infallible. She would rather admit her own shortcomings than to disappoint a young lady who wanted to sing.

I am not saying that the details of etiquette are to be overlooked. No one can completely ignore these things, but Mrs. Post has taken care of this subject beautifully. Any and all may polish up on what to do. Personality relieves the tenseness when you discover you forgot to do the right thing! I know that we should attend to all the little details before the party, but we are all guilty of oversight now and then; and I do insist that charm and personality are entirely aside and apart from conventional, orthodox "do's" and "don't's" in regard to who sits where, or who speaks first.

Let's take a typical day of Mme. Garrigue's life, in order to grasp the fullness and richness of her days. She rises early, and the first thing when she awakes, she asks of Infinite Intelligence, "What shall I do today?" This is with the thought of doing something aside from her routine duties. The day is started with a clear mind, with the expectation of doing a little good before the day is gone. Then before breakfast, she walks to church. Breakfast over, she starts with her lessons, teaching until mid-afternoon. This behind her, there is always some former student who comes by for a visit, or a bit of advice about the work at hand, the future, or the voice. She keeps up with them all, writes to them, lives their joys and their sorrows. Every day is full, busy, and constructive.

The spirit in which one does things for others is the greatest reflection of that individual's personality. Remember, the important thing is the spirit in which one does things for another!

The most deadening poison in the world to any personality is idleness. Lack of interest in a program, no definite plans, no definite aims and ambitions will kill all possibility of charm. This is the negative side of life, and if indulged will build selfishness, pettiness, futility, and loneliness. We reflect in our very personality exactly the thoughts we think and the emotions in our hearts. And, without exception, the thoughts we have, the feelings and emotions in our hearts are, in fact, a part of us. There is no escaping this! We build for ourselves futures filled with rich friendships, with full, happy lives; or we face barren walls and loneliness. Just what we find in our future lies entirely within ourselves.

What we find in our future lies entirely within ourselves.

The most outstanding contrast I know to Mme. Garrigue and her remarkable life is another friend of mine—twenty years younger in actual numbers of years. She is active in business, has executive ability, and is now holding a position of responsibility. The last time I saw her, she was talking about when the time came, she hoped she would be able to get a black dress and a hundred dollars—the requirements for entrance in the Old Ladies Home.

This is a woman with twenty years advantage over Mme. Garrigue, and who will find herself living in the Old Ladies Home long before another twenty years have passed. Why? Not because there is any need for it, but because she is hopelessly lost in a negative rut of destructive thinking, building for her future a place in the Old Ladies Home.

It has not been many years since women felt they could not admit the age of forty. Horrors! One was old at forty! I am of the opinion the Duchess of Windsor has broken the record for being attractive after forty. She has crippled the chances of the little shilly-shallow youngsters when it comes to being attractive. Men have all begun to look around. Pretty faces and youth are no longer in vogue. Today any man, whether he be sixteen or sixty, is looking for a polished sophisticate who possesses poise, charm, and finesse; not for a pretty face that babbles baby talk and knows nothing of the current topics of the day.

When we consider personality from the analytical viewpoint, break it down and study its component parts, we find there is a definite plan for developing personality, whether we are young or well up the ladder of years. The various things to be done all rest entirely within our power; things we, ourselves control—or can control—all within our own mind, excepting the least important which is personal appearance, and even that may be controlled within the limits of one's income. But the most important part of any woman is her personality, not her appearance, not her race, creed, looks, or her age.

> *The most important part of any woman is her personality, not her appearance, not her race, creed, looks, or her age.*

One of the most charming women I know happens to be my cook. Helen is a large person; she is a marvelous cook, yes, but when she greets you with a broad smile, and finds ways and means of cheering you up if things have not been going just right, she is no longer "just a good cook." She sings in the kitchen and beams all over anyone who goes back there, never grumbling when there is someone extra for dinner, or when the meal is a bit delayed, or we are irregular coming in to dinner. Helen has charm, she has friends, she is remembered by everyone who comes into contact with her. Yet Helen is just a cook.

When a cook can make herself so much a part of the household, consider how many young women in business fail to make themselves a necessary part of the job. Most of the girls who work, work for so much money each payday. That is all they get out of it. But more of working later—it is too important to skip over lightly.

The object of this chapter is to discuss the mind, the things we think, the things we feel. Everything is first built within the mind. This is a known fact. An architect must plan every detail of a house in his mind before a single stone is turned. A cook must know in her own mind just what she wants, cake or bread, before she begins the mixture. A dressmaker must picture in her mind just what the dress will be before she cuts the cloth.

Just as tangible things are built within the mind, so is a personality built within the mind of the individual concerned. The personality will be positive, attractive, magnetic, and charming if the mind is kept clean of negative thoughts. The personality will be negative, unattractive, repulsive, and selfish if the mind is allowed to feed on the weeds of negative thoughts.

Consequently, we are faced with the study of positive and negative thinking. Let's take up the negative side first. What are negative thoughts? There are so many, but I believe the strongest and most dominant in women would come under the heading of futility, or self-pity.

So many women arrive at maturity entirely without any plans, even though they may have married. They have not planned a definite pattern for life. If they have not married, they are aimlessly drifting around as a ship tosses about on the ocean. Most women who work, just work. They do not build a career of their work. They do not plan for the future beyond a pittance for security, or a burial fund which has been set aside. Thus they drift into self-pity, self-sympathy, and the weeds of this nature grow rapidly; soon they are hopelessly choked with the pettiness of life. Life consists of neighborhood gossip, just what Mrs. Jones is doing, or Miss Smith, or the neighbor's children, and such inconsequential small talk. How could they hope to be attractive women?

If I call on you, I do not want to hear all the troubles you are having with your husband, or your children, or about the scraps of your neighbors and relatives. I want to talk about things that are constructive, things which build positive thinking, for I have disciplined my mind to feed on positive thoughts and to refuse negatives. I would be exceedingly interested in knowing that you are working with your son toward his career as an artist, an aviator, or even just a bookkeeper; that you have built a dream-house in your mind, that you have accumulated enough to buy the land, and in another five or ten years you will be ready to place that dream-house into brick and mortar. I would be interested to know that you are actually working toward some definite end, with a goal, a purpose behind every day; that each day has given you something. I would be keenly interested in knowing about the children you have helped, the unfortunate boy you are sending to camp, the Jones family who needed help, and how you went to their aid and helped them through a tough spot.

If you cannot be constructive in your thoughts you can never be constructive in your heart. Unless you are constructive in your heart, sincerely desirous of helping, you can never hope to build a charming, magnetic, attractive personality. This is just as true as the fact that the sun cannot shine when there is a heavy raincloud over it.

And, the sun will never shine until the raincloud has been removed; then, and then only, do we get the rays of the sun, the cheerfulness and beauty of the sunlight.

The place to start improving your personality is not in the dress shop and the beauty parlor, but right in your own heart, and the only key to your heart lies in your own conscious mind. Note that I say your conscious mind. Your heart is the reflection of your subconscious mind, and is what it is because of the food (thoughts) you have been feeding it all these years. If your heart is small, selfish, and petty, it is because you have lived with thoughts of that nature so long they have taken root in your very heart.

However, it is also possible for you to plow them under, and plant the flower garden you would so like to have in your heart. It is possible for you—and only you—to make the change.

How?

By thinking the positive thoughts and living positive deeds. And what are positive thoughts? Positive thoughts always build, not only for self, but chiefly for others. If you have found your heart a weed-patch, it is my suggestion that you use as a plow to turn under the weeds one simple practice; make a habit of doing something for someone else every day. Do something that will make another happy—and do it solely for that purpose.

Sit down and write a letter to your mother who has been wanting to hear from you.

Pick a few flowers and call on the little old lady who lives alone down the street and is so lonely for company.

Help anyone and everyone, and above everything else, if you cannot say something nice, something good about a person, say nothing at all! This may enforce a week or so of silence upon you, if you have the bad habit of gossiping; but it will also show you just how ugly your own personality has grown.

This is the plow, the starting point at turning under the weeds that have accumulated. If applied earnestly and consistently over a period of time, all the weeds will wither away, and you will find that you get much more pleasure out of the new friends and the new self you have built than you ever did as a selfish, disgruntled woman.

Remember, this is the starting point. I know it is radical. I know you will say "I can't afford it," or "I haven't the time," but just as surely as you say that, you are pandering to yourself, and building a negative personality, for none of us use to best advantage even half of the twenty-four hours allotted to us each day.

This is step number one, and incidentally, the most important of all is the starting; the clearing away of stumps and stones, the plowing under of the weeds, and the fertilization of the soil in order that we may plan and build a lovely garden spot in which to live.

CHAPTER 3

Find Something Definite to Do

There is an old saying, "An idle mind is the Devil's workshop." Truer words were never spoken. It is astonishing to discover how many women have absolutely nothing to do from dawn until dark, the whole week through. That is, nothing constructive; nothing that really matters.

Perhaps, sometime during the day the average woman must think about what will be served for dinner, or maybe one or two days during the week she must go to Sally's bridge party, or to the Missionary meeting, or the Garden Club—but then, it doesn't make a great deal of difference whether or not she goes, for after all, it's not so very important.

The woman does not live who doesn't need something to do; and by that I mean something very definite in the way of a plan, some activity which is actually a part of the woman herself, and which will consume her sincere interest and activity.

Every woman needs to prepare herself for business while she is gathering an education, and I feel that every woman should have at least one year of actual experience in the business world, actively engaged in some useful occupation, and earning her way in the world. She needs this in order that she may have a better understanding when the time comes that her husband comes in tired and worn out, and does not feel like putting on his new suit and going to a party. She can understand an upside-down day at the office or shop only after she has had a few of them on her own account. She can understand the fluctuations of business and income much better if she has had the experience of managing on a self-earned salary. She understands only after she has earned her own money there are exactly 100 cents in every one of Uncle Sam's dollars, whether the statisticians proclaim 49 or a 149, and she knows just how to get 100 cents out of the dollar she spends.

There are many women who believe they are hopelessly lost in the commercial world, because they have had no business training, or because they feel they are too old to begin. This is not true. There is work for any woman who really wants it.

There is work for any woman who really wants it.

Business can no longer get along without women, and some firms offer wonderful opportunities, limited only by the individual's capabilities and willingness to work. It is no disgrace today for a woman to work. In fact, a woman is rather admired and respected when she makes a place for herself in business, especially when she makes a success of her venture.

May I offer a word of advice to every mother of a young girl? If you have a daughter starting out in life, whether you have trained her only through high school, or through the highest college of learning–unless you have given her an actual business course in practical business training, you have not given her the most essential part of her education! Before any girl (or for that matter, any boy), goes to college, she should have shorthand and typewriting! I know, because

I did not get this training until after I had finished college, and then I found out how much I needed these things while in college! Any career upon which a girl may launch herself will be aided by the practical use of shorthand and typing, for these things are marketable in any field!

These suggestions, of course, are offered for those who have not passed the willingness to begin, who have not entirely given up the idea of living. If you have given up the idea of doing something in the commercial world, there is still one rule which you must follow—find something else to do and do it!

But what can you do? There are so many things one can do. If nothing else, you could systematically knit with a definite purpose behind your knitting. I would put this at the bottom of the list, if your health is so far gone that exercise and physical activity are entirely out of the question.

It might not be a bad idea to begin looking around for the benefit of your friends and neighbors, or your own immediate family. There are countless things you can do right at home. If you are a woman who loves the out-of-doors, and games, such as tennis, golf, or hiking in the woods, just think what wonderful times could be had if you would organize the kids in the neighborhood and take them on hikes, gathering facts about nature, learning more about your own community and nature's wonders. Just think what it would do for the youngsters!

If you are musically inclined, you could teach a few of the youngsters who cannot afford to take professional instructions. Build a neighborhood orchestra; it would keep you busy, give you something to do, and certainly would make you the village heroine.

If you are an excellent cook, there are always things for you to do. It seems those who love to cook find excuses to join church luncheon groups and other cook organizations which keep them occupied.

If you understand boys and have one of your own who is at that age when all boys are a question mark, you could interest him and his friends in forming a little club, you to furnish them with the garage, barn, or basement for the headquarters, and help them plan various expeditions and enterprises, actually entering into the spirit with them. You would not only be doing them a great deal of good, but you would be surprised to discover the change that came over yourself.

This business of finding something to do, unless you are definitely employed in a position which holds your sustained interest, is generally best solved by the application of the advice given in a previous chapter—do something for someone else every day that comes along, work out a plan whereby you can do this; the day will seem brighter, and soon you will find the difference in yourself for which you have been praying.

In connection with those who are regularly employed in a job, do not think occupation eight hours of the day automatically justifies the other sixteen hours and makes them entirely happy and undisturbed. Not at all! The first thing to consider is—why are you working? What do you think of your job? What do you think of the people with whom you work? These things seem to shock you. I thought so—you see, I used to work, and I know something of what office routine can be. I know some of the pettiness among the employees in any office or department store, but this need not trouble you if you do a little cleaning of your own house. That house is, as ever, in the thoughts you think, and the spirit in which you work.

Do you go to the office in the morning thinking, "My heavens! Another day in that stuffy old place! And Mr. Brown! The old crab! I wish he would go jump in the lake!" You see, it is just this frame of mind which causes Mr. Brown to bawl you out when you get there. I can't explain it, but people actually pick up our thoughts, our state of mind, and reflect these thoughts right back to us in both attitude and spoken words.

As the day proceeds, do you keep your eye on the clock, and think about the date you have tonight, or are you interested in the work you are doing? Do you think this irrelevant? Indeed it is not, for thereupon hinges your worth to your job—and to yourself. Thereupon hinges the very possibility of your ever being happy, for if you have so little interest in your job the chances are you will have as little interest in your husband, your home, and your children when those things are added to your life; they will be heavy on your hands, for you do not love life. You do not love to live. You are what is commonly called a chronic complainer—and if there is one of these in the world who has a dozen friends, that, within itself constitutes a world's wonder.

It is unwise for a woman to do work she does not like, and for which she is unsuited. As an example of this, I shall make a confession (one which will probably shock many good housewives): I do not like to cook, keep house, or do any of the domestic things which most women adore—yet I like a lovely home. Consequently, before I married, I pointed out these shortcomings to my husband—he took me, shortcomings and all. What do I do with my time? I work right with my husband, though my work does not claim definite hours and schedules. I sit at one typewriter and write while my husband sits at another, and we work together. The house takes care of itself, and we both are exceptionally happy.

I am not the only woman who dislikes housework, and for these women, I suggest that they continue work after marriage, in such lines as make them happy. Let me warn you against just working, allowing the money to go into the general fund. Work with a definite plan and a definite purpose for your money. Live on your husband's income and take yours, buy Government bonds, real estate, or such other properties and securities as will prove sound investments for the future, both your own and your children's. In this way the effort is not wasted.

This plan may not fit in with the rules of a generation ago, but after all, we are not living a generation ago—we are living today and tomorrow, so let's face the things that exist today and tomorrow. One of these is the change of the place of women in society. In Grandmother's day, she was so busy with a dozen children and the problems concerning the immediate family and neighbors, that time was at a premium. Grandmother lived to a ripe old age and was a happy woman until the children grew up and she found herself with nothing to do.

The family has dwindled. Modern inventions have altered house-keeping, made it a matter of pressing a few buttons and pushing a few gadgets about—then, what to do with the rest of the day? If you play bridge, that is all right if you like it, but if that is your main interest, play hard, and play consistently. Personally, I think it is pretty much a waste of time, but if it keeps you busy and happy, then play bridge.

There is no church in the land that does not need to have some work done. Work concerning the immediate church group, actually helping the people of the community. Keep doing something.

Most women really need something very definite in the way of a working program; something which will contribute financially, for we are not yet over the shock of the Depression. There are many fields open to women today, and many firms offer wonderful opportunities to women—that is, to women who really want to get ahead.

Of course, the most ideal method of working is the position where you can control your own hours and establish your contacts and following. There are various ways of making affiliations of this nature with reliable firms, and with little or no investment to be made. You probably know of some but just never realized you needed something to do with yourself and your time.

Forming a definite plan of work, I would say is the harrowing of the ground, preparatory to sowing the seed of a charming personality, for without this step (something to do), it is hard to develop the first requisite of charm, which is poise.

CHAPTER 4

Poise

*J*ust what is poise? *Webster* defines it as "weight; balance; equilibrium." That does not mean two hundred pounds balanced on two feet. It means the ability to face anyone, king or pauper, under any circumstance, without becoming "rattled."

And how does one acquire this ability? By first, last, and always being one's self. Perhaps the best illustration available to explain just exactly what I mean is the late Will Rogers. A mere gum-chewing cow puncher from Oklahoma, he met kings, queens, presidents, premiers, and celebrities by the score. How did he behave? What did he do? What did he say? He behaved just as he would with you or me, said the things that popped into his mind, and did the things natural to Will Rogers. There was nothing false about him.

Poise is impossible without naturalness. Sham, pretense, and affectation destroy self-confidence, make one uncertain, and therefore are the enemies of poise—yet poise is thoroughly essential in the development of personality. A woman without poise is as hopelessly lost when it comes to making a favorable impression as if she were not there at all. This is well worth remembering. It is impossible to make a favorable impression on strangers without a certain amount of poise.

There are certain things which one may do in order to build poise. Poise which consists purely of self-confidence, and self-control.

Perhaps the fact that you have not had the opportunity to mix with others, to hold the lime-light is the cause of your self-consciousness. If this is the case, it is my suggestion that you begin immediately to do something about it. Join a group which is made up of strangers, or at least others than your regular acquaintances and friends; perhaps a little theatre group or a public speaking class, or something which will cause you to stand on your feet and talk in front of people whom you do not know, and before whom you are not at home and comfortable.

A little theatre group may be the most satisfactory arrangement for this. These groups are formed in almost every community, and if there is none in your city, it would behoove you to start it. Certainly the youngsters—your own sons and daughters if you have some—need the experience in order that they may grow up with the very quality you are seeking.

There are many ways in which one may gain poise, by building self-confidence and mastering self-control. But it can never be done by just thinking about it. This is one thing that must be put into action, worked on consistently and regularly with determination.

Most people who lack poise are those who have lived within certain limited circles all their lives. Once removed from the old friends and the familiar ground of home and neighborhood, they become completely overwhelmed. This is rather akin to the feeling when you first approach a city in some foreign country and suddenly realize you cannot speak the language, nor do you know anything about the place. There is a "sinking" feeling; but in a strange place, you at least have the privilege of being alone, and because of this you force yourself to take the problem in hand and work your way out of the situation.

Travel is always a help in overcoming the lack of poise. The constant meeting of strange people in new places automatically gives one the ability to meet strangers with ease. But your bank account may not allow a great amount of travel for the purpose of gaining poise, so let's consider the methods available right in your own backyard.

First, do you have any particular talent which can be exhibited? Say that you dance nicely, or sing, or play some musical instrument. If this is the case, the matter is easily solved. Gather about you some group who are also talented, and join the little theatre group who are struggling to become thespians. Or form a little dance club of several couples and meet at different places for a social evening of dancing.

If you do not have any talent, you may participate in church work, or school work—join a group and take an active interest. By active interest, I mean actually participate, stand on your feet and talk, just pitch in and talk. If you have nothing to say, find something to say, then stand on your feet and say it. At first your throat may seem dry, and you may become rattled a bit, but after a few "flops" you will find that it is not so difficult, and soon you will be leading the meeting.

The literary clubs are also good places to get in this sort of practice, or teaching Sunday school, or any one of a dozen civic and social clubs and organizations all of which are open to you. All organizations are delighted to have active and interested members.

There is one thing you may as well recognize—neither you nor anyone else will ever gain poise by trying to "put on the dog." This habit of using broken dishes and ragged table linens on the kitchen table thirty days a month is out of the question. When company comes, you get out the fine china, the nice linens, and set a formal table. Of course, you are going to upset the coffee. Junior is going to pull some smart crack about the "swell feed," or inquire into "where'd you get the swanky silverware and the pretty dishes?" John is going to fuss because he has to wear his coat when the weather is so hot—and neither you nor your company will enjoy the dinner.

I suggest a little compromise by way of building poise for yourself—and your family. Perhaps you cannot afford to use the best that you have every day. Most people do not like to use the finest for everyday, but it costs no more to set an attractive table than an unattractive one—not with the ten-cent stores at every corner with every conceivable housekeeping aid for almost nothing.

A little formality every day, such as making Junior behave just as if there were company, and serving attractive meals with a little frill will prevent such tragedies. These things take very little more time or trouble, and the effect is certainly worth the effort. You feel better, your husband enjoys his dinner more, and Junior grows up a gentleman of good manners rather than an impossible and uncontrollable concern at the dinner table.

So many women who have the responsibility of molding the lives of children are thoughtless and careless of the inhibitions and complexes they are building in their children. Perhaps you are suffering from the lack of poise, or from some other inhibition because of home outgrowth of your childhood. Did your big sister make you stay in the background? Did your mother scold you in public? Did someone publicly embarrass you? Were you treated as a grown-up? Did you eat with the family, as one of them—and were the same good table manners demanded of you that were demanded of the adults—or was the dinner table a battle ground for a family scrap?

These things can cause lasting handicaps. Complexes are subtle, and sometimes very deep. People do not always recognize the fact that they possess a complex; but chances are an old, or some more recent inhibition, is the thing which makes you refrain from taking an active part in the Parent-Teachers, the Garden Club, or other social organizations. Again, may I emphasize just what an active interest means—it is actually participating in the program. If you feel shy, force yourself to do something inconspicuous at first; gradually begin to take part in the meetings until you learn to stand on your feet and speak, and speak whenever there is an opportunity.

This is the best antidote for the lack of poise that I know, excepting the meeting of strangers in the role of hostess, where the burden lies squarely on your shoulders. The best way to break into this practice is to make it a point at every meeting of your club to speak to at least three strangers—or if there are no absolute strangers present, speak to three with whom you are not well acquainted. No "how-do-you-do" is sufficient; you must converse with them, force yourself to be friendly.

After you have limbered up on these little tricks, then you may take the next step, and you will be surprised to find just how you have improved. The next step is to actually invite some of the people you have met in your new circle, or if you can, the entire group for tea; tea is inexpensive and delightfully informal.

Just take yourself in hand and force yourself through these few steps persistently, and you will find your old self-consciousness

Poise is the outgrowth of self-assurance.

disappearing. The new friendships and acquaintances, plus the newly gained poise, will more than make up for the first few panicky times that your knees trembled and your voice cracked when you faced a stranger.

There is no better way of overcoming the lack of poise than through self-expression. Poise is the outgrowth of self-assurance. This can be gained only after a great deal of self-expression. So, if you would gain poise, force yourself to participate in social, civic, literary clubs, or in theatrical groups.

Many are apt to feel despondent and become
discouraged in the work of self-culture, because they do
not get on in the world so fast as they deserve to do;
having planted their acorn, they expect to
see it grow into an oak at once.

CHAPTER 5

Sincerity of Purpose

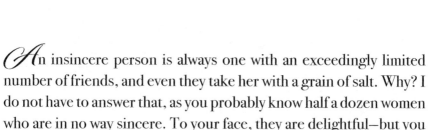

An insincere person is always one with an exceedingly limited number of friends, and even they take her with a grain of salt. Why? I do not have to answer that, as you probably know half a dozen women who are in no way sincere. To your face, they are delightful—but you dare not turn your back!

It is so easy to slip into this exceedingly bad habit. We do this by just petty back-yard chit-chat until we have formed the habit of seeking gossip in order to spread the news. We become chummy with Mrs. Jones in order to get the "dirt" to tell to Mrs. Smith and the rest of the crowd.

Now please understand there is a big difference between a sincere interest in Mrs. Jones and her troubles, and a meddlesome curiosity regarding the same thing.

Where does the difference lie? In your own heart. If you are sincerely interested, you will help Mrs. Jones in her trouble rather than rush to spread the news of her misfortunes.

There are many women who seem to get real joy out of hearing gossip, and even more in telling others the "news." This is not true just of the women who are not busy—it is just as true of those who work in the offices and business houses.

I intend to give no dissertation on the evils of gossip, but I do intend to show just how easily anyone can slip into dangerous habits by even listening to such talk. It is seldom that a woman will admit she is a busy-body, for nearly every gossiper precedes almost every choice morsel with the remark, "Now you know, I never gossip or talk about anyone, but"—and then comes the dishing of the dirt.

Why bring this out? Simply for the reason that the only person in the world the gossiper is kidding is herself. She does not know she's a gossip. That is the truth—for she has never met her true self. It would pay us all to form the habit of sitting down at least once a day and taking a look into our hearts. What horrible things some of us would discover!

In our home, my husband and I have a habit which has proven most beneficial and has absolutely cured us, forever, of insincerity or ever saying anything against anyone, and has taught us to search for a kind word to say of everyone. We analyze the happenings of each day as it goes by. Sometimes we do this at night, sometimes in the morning. We analyze ourselves and acknowledge to each other our short-comings—not in a fault-finding way, but for the purpose of learning more about ourselves as people. After all, we are in the business of studying and helping people, and it fits into our work program; but the greatest thing it has done is it has checked us up, and made us more careful of what we say—and of what we think of others.

Once you have admitted the possibility of this weakness, you want to know what to do to make yourself absolutely sincere of purpose. Of course, gossip is not the only crime of insincerity, but it is probably the most vicious, and the most damaging to one's self, so let's start with that particular thing.

The best thing to do is to sit down with yourself, make a complete list of all the people you know whom you do not like, then force yourself to find some good points—as many as possible—which you can honestly recognize in each one. Forget all the things you do not like; you have taken care of these already. List every good point these people have, memorize them, and the very next time you see these people, or someone who knows them, say something complimentary of them.

Ah! but that's being a hypocrite, you say. Well, if you have gotten so deep into bad habits that you must be a hypocrite to say something truthful, then it's high time you started to work on yourself.

At this point it is well to remember we believe the things we repeat.

Our minds feed upon the thoughts we feed them—and even though we do not actually believe this or that, with constant repetition we can convince ourselves and reach the point of belief. So—is it not better to sow constructive thoughts and ideas, than to plant destructive ones? For we take on the earmarks of the thoughts we think just as surely as we are burned by the sun and chilled by the snows.

You are now beginning to plant the seed in your own mind for the purpose of building constructive thought habits. Good habits are built by the method of repetition just as surely as are destructive habits. By saying and thinking complimentary things, you will find yourself losing the dislikes and prejudices you once held.

Because every person should fully realize it, I repeat: we are a perfect picture of the thoughts we think. Every move we make, every word we utter, even the tone of the voice, the look in the eye, the expression of the face is a reflection of the thoughts with which we live.

If we have drifted into bad thinking habits, then it is best that we set about systematically cleaning house. The best way to clean house is to do it every day, until the whole mess has been cleared away. Take hold of yourself, force yourself to find something good and kind in every person you see. If you cannot say something nice about another, then just keep your mouth shut—say nothing! If you catch yourself thinking unkind thoughts, start thinking of something else. Do not allow the negative thoughts to accumulate in your mind, for thoughts are like people—they attract unto them others of the same nature.

Thoughts are like people—they attract unto them others of the same nature.

You would hardly expect to find royalty sleeping in the gutter with a drunken bum; neither would you be apt to find clean, constructive thoughts wallowing in the mire and mud of an unclean mind. Any mind that tolerates negative thoughts is unclean and the worst enemy of its owner.

The subject of sincerity of purpose is so closely related to, and dependent upon, positive thought, that I am going further in order that you may develop some system or plan by which you can learn to control your thoughts, and thus control your nature, personality, and disposition.

Incidentally, a person's disposition has a great deal to do with their personality. I know several women who do not have such charm and magnetism as would allow one to say they have outstanding personalities, but their wonderful dispositions make up for the lack of magnetism. After all, we must live with our dispositions, and even worse, our families must live with us!

Really the greatest tragedy of all is that we have spent so little time in being decent with our relatives, particularly those who live in the house with us. This is really something we should consider. Father will spend thousands of dollars for a fine house. Mother will spend thousands for clothes. Brother will spend hundreds on the girls, and sister will be "peaches and cream" when the boys call—but just let company leave the house, and the fur flies in every direction. Why? Just because we seem to have no consideration for those who live in the house with us, when the truth is, we should have more consideration for them than anyone else in the world.

The habits we build around the house become a definite part of our character and our personality. Of all the bad habits we have, perhaps the worst is nagging. This is not entirely confined to Mother, but she is just as guilty as Father or any of the others. If Betty wants to wear a red dress, Mother thinks a blue one would be better—why? "Just because!" What better reason is there than the old stand-by, "just because"?

When Father comes in from his work tired, and mother has had a delightful time with the children—they've been fighting all day—she starts in on him with a barrage of questions that make no particular difference; then he flies back at her with unkind remarks, and there, before dinner, is a beautiful scrap.

If you really want to check up on yourself before you decide you are not guilty of nagging, I would suggest that you hesitate before you say or ask anything of another, and ask yourself this question, "Would I want someone to ask that of me?" If you do that you will be in a better position to get at the truth about your habits of nagging. Nagging is a thoroughly destructive habit, it does no one any good, and it does a great deal of damage to all, particularly to yourself, in that it allows you to fall into the habit of fault-finding and negative thinking. Again may I emphasize the habit of thinking? There is nothing in the world so important to any individual as the habit of positive thinking, developed and exercised!

If your thinking habits have become negative through carelessness, then the best thing to do is to begin making positive thoughts your business until such time as you have developed positive thought-habits.

If you would like to nag, to make some petty dig at Father, or Betty, or the next-door neighbor, stop and look for something else to say. Tell Father that he looks good, that Mrs. Jones was just saying what a handsome man he is. Tell Betty that she looks particularly nice in the dress she is wearing, or that her hair looks nice today. If you can't think of anything nice to say, discuss the weather. If that brings up an argument, just refrain from talking until you get yourself absolutely under control.

If there is anything worse than nagging and gossiping, it is the habit of complaining. This is positively the world's worst offence. If you have a complaint to make, just stop and check up on yourself, see how many complaints you register during the course of the day, then add them up for the week, then for the month, then for the year—and just take a look at the staggering figure. It is unbelievable that a person could be so disagreeable! But you have been guilty, and by your own admission.

You may wonder what complaints have to do with sincerity of purpose. Did you ever stop to consider the real reason for a complaint? It is seldom the reason given on the surface. Some people complain of ill health, not because they are really ill, but because they are too lazy to work, or because they want attention. It is very difficult to get to the bottom of the real cause for complaints. You can rest assured there is something at the bottom of the complaint which is a selfish streak exercising this as a means to an end. Even though it is your own complaint, you are the last person in the world to stop and analyze the real cause, and the motive behind it.

In checking up on yourself in regard to complaints, do not kid yourself; count all the complaints to the servants, to the children, to your neighbors, to yourself, to your husband, your mother, your father, to everyone. This is a habit we drift into by way of self-pity, or sometimes by seeking a bit of attention. How much better it would be for us to seek attention by saying and doing things which interest the person to whom we are talking, than by bothering him with complaints.

Most complaints center around the house, the family, or one's self; in this case it is generally in relation to health. This is something with which I am sure doctors will agree; most of the women who complain of this, that, and the other illness only have a case of negative thinking which is not curable by any physician unless he is a psychologist and can take a strong hold on the mind of the woman concerned. It is exceedingly difficult for a doctor to do this, for if he does not tell her that she is really ill, then she seeks another doctor, until she finds some quack who will agree with her, charge outrageous fees, and pander to her whims.

This type of woman is a perfect nuisance; she is good for spoiling any party, she always has a story of some operation, or illness to tell, some new pain, some fancy disease which has the doctors baffled.

On the other hand, do not go around telling people how terrible they look, asking what is the matter with them. This is just as bad to do this as to complain yourself—even worse, for you are sowing the seed of negative thought in the mind of another, contaminating another, which is more dangerous than sowing the seed in your own mind.

I was greatly impressed with this at a time when it was vitally necessary to keep my aunt buoyed up in her own mind. She had just gone through a terrible time in the hospital, and only by the strength of her own will and the skill of the surgeon did she pull through. She was out of danger, and at home. An old girlhood friend had been trying to see her ever since she went to the hospital, but we had cautioned everyone against letting this woman in, because of her unfortunate habit of saying the wrong thing every time.

After my aunt came home, the old friend dropped in to "cheer her up" and during the greetings, she carne out with the remark, "Well, Kate, it seems to me anybody who got as close to the grave as you, should have made a go of it." This may be funny in print, where there is nothing at stake, but it was not funny to my aunt who was only questionably safe from the grave even then.

See what negative, destructive thinking can do? Just as we kept that woman away from my aunt for months, other people will avoid you if you are a hypochondriac—they must in self-defense.

It is impossible to overcome the constant drumming of negative thoughts from other people. Rather than subject one's self to negative thoughts, it is better to avoid the people who make such unwise remarks.

There is another form of negative thinking which may come under the general head of complaints, but it is slightly different for most people admit they are guilty, adding immediately, they cannot help it. If you cannot help the thoughts you think, then you cannot help anything else—for the mind, your own mind is the only thing in the world over which you may have control.

This is worry. Some women worry, and are rather proud of the fact. If they have no troubles of their own, they borrow some from friends. This is a peculiar bent that some people seem to follow, but it is none the less true. It is a deadening factor, once it is allowed to take root, for it builds the negative, and destroys the positive side of life entirely. Why? Simply because positive thoughts and negative thoughts are never bedfellows, and where there is worry, there can never be a positive mind.

Worries come in two classifications: one, the things over which we have no control. These we may dismiss because if we have no control over them, obviously we can do nothing about them. Two, the things over which we have control. These are useless worries built up entirely within our own minds.

If the thing we are worrying about is within our own control, then we should do something about it, correct the situation and dismiss the annoyance of the worry. If you have no control over it, certainly worry will do no good.

Now you will come back at me and say, "That's easier said than done." Surely you do not think it is impossible for you to do this if you really want to be rid of the worry. Again I ask you to check up with yourself and find out if you know exactly what you want. Some people actually enjoy a good worry, and always have several around. But if you do not worry for the pleasure it gives you, then put your mind to work on something entirely removed from the subject about which you are worrying, something which is constructive.

"Why?" you ask. I may answer by asking you a question. Do you know what worry does to your personality, to your personal appearance? If you recognized this, you would never tolerate a worry, not even for a second.

Worry brings upon one a thoroughly negative, repulsive nature which destroys any magnetism of personality that may have ever been present. It also puts lines of a most damaging effect into the face. It deadens the eyes to a dull, lifeless appearance. It gives one a nervousness which is most annoying to all who are around. It puts wrinkles in the face, turns the corners of the mouth down, and gives one a "haggard" expression. It is the most deadly of all the weapons woman may use against herself, for it is the Perfect Destroyer.

Then what am I to do? You are to give yourself a course in self-discipline in constructive thinking, consisting of four things:

First: Find nice things to say about everyone—and say them.

Second: Think before making any remark that may border on nagging.

Third: Never make a complaint, either to yourself or anyone else.

Fourth: Train your mind to think of subjects not connected with your pet worry.

CHAPTER 6

Harmony

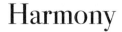

$\mathcal{T}$he subject of harmony within self—and with others—is one of the most important factors in any woman's life. It is so essential that the lack of harmony may easily destroy a woman's usefulness, her personality, or her career. This goes not only for women, but for men as well.

The point is to recognize just where, and what is the cause for the lack of harmony. Ask yourself these questions: "Exactly where does the lack of harmony lie? Within myself? Within my associates? Within my work? Within my family?" It is bound to lie in one of these places, and you are best fitted to judge for yourself just where—provided, of course, you are honest with yourself.

Once this problem is settled, then ask these questions: "What is the cause of this lack of harmony? Is it because of myself? Is it because of my associates? Is it because of my work? Is it because of my family?"

Seek the real cause of this lack of harmony, and you are ready to begin searching for the ways and means of eliminating it. This will vary with each set of circumstances; therefore, it is impossible for me to give any set rule of procedure. But I might offer a few suggestions. For instance, if it is revealed (by honest analysis) that the lack of harmony lies within yourself, of course, you must begin to reconstruct the habits of thought which will automatically eliminate the trouble.

If it is discovered that the lack of harmony comes from some member of your associates who does not agree with your ambitions and ideals, then it is very simple; drop that associate, and the trouble is ended.

If the trouble lies within your job, your work, this requires even more analysis. First you should determine if you like the kind of work you are doing. Ask yourself if you like the firm (the personnel) for which you work; then, do you like your immediate superiors? For example, an artist at heart, who lives for the development of individual creative work, could never work satisfactorily and happily in a mechanical position where every day is the same as every other day. A person who loves detailed routine would be miserable in an executive position. These things should be carefully studied as they relate to your own particular case, and worked out accordingly.

If you reach the verdict that your work is not suited to you, then the best thing to do is to find the line of work that is best suited, and go to it. This will eliminate the trouble quickly. Do not tell me that suitable work cannot be had—work can be had by anyone who desires it and who fits herself for it.

Say that the lack of harmony comes from some member of your immediate family. This makes it quite difficult at times, for after all, we do have the privilege of choosing our associates, work, and friends, but none of us have any choice of relatives. However, for that very reason, we do not have to tolerate them if they stand in our way and make life miserable for us, excepting of course, the children we have brought into the world. If it is a child of yours which is causing the disharmony, then there are obligations on your part which must be taken into consideration. Other relatives such as parents, aunts, uncles, cousins, and "family pride" (which is generally false and worthless) are beyond your control, and can be as easily cast aside as associates.

However, it is always well to look a dozen times toward yourself before you decide upon whom lies the burden of blame for the lack of harmony. In nearly every case, you will find it entirely within yourself. By this, I mean your state of mind, your habits of thought, your self-pity, your self-interest, or your strong minded determination to go through with something that is not for your own best interests.

Sometimes we are easily blinded by our desire to take the limelight, to do something to cause talk among our friends, our family, and our associates, and these little caprices often are too costly for the pleasure of fleeting conversation.

It is well to look within ourselves for our own salvation; to search right there for the answer. We, after all, can control only ourselves. Never can we control or be sure of the reactions of another; therefore, it is risky business to depend too greatly upon Uncle John reacting exactly as we expect when we try to pull his leg for a trip to Europe or a job at the factory.

Harmony within yourself can come only after careful analysis of yourself, your job, your home relations, and your social relations, and a recognition of just who needs straightening out. Generally, it lies within your own mind to do a little adjusting. This is fortunate, for we can always adjust the thing we control, and we do still possess the right to control our own mind.

In discussing harmony, it is essential to emphasize the importance of self-discipline. This quality is probably the most important factor in anyone's make-up. It is essential because in proportion to the degree of self-control and self-discipline we exercise, stand the chances of getting ahead in any field, from making friends to succeeding in business and in the home.

When you allow any habit to get so entrenched that you "cannot break it" the time has come to take yourself in hand and master yourself. When you lose your temper, when you become lax and without system in keeping house, the time has come when you must do something about it. When you find yourself without rigid self- discipline in regard to your work, it is futile to hope for advancement, or increase in income.

It is unfortunate that women do not have the privilege of military training, for this is the greatest and most efficient teacher of self-discipline yet devised. But not having this, we must seek other methods of training ourselves in this most essential quality. How? There are many ways. You may assign yourself certain duties to be done at certain times—regardless of your mood at the moment, and force yourself to follow through on them.

For instance, you may lay a program for the week, planning to write certain overdue letters on Monday; calling on someone who is ill on Tuesday; repairing the seams, snaps, and snags in your wardrobe on Wednesday; cleaning the guest room spick and span on Thursday; giving yourself a good manicure on Friday; and laying plans for next week's menus on Saturday. This is only suggested, the idea being that you force yourself to do things designated on the appointed day. None of these things will take all day, and none will deprive you of your regular routine for long.

There are other ways—and one very good one is to make yourself attend to your face every night, regardless of how tired you may feel, or how indisposed you may be. This is a most profitable way in which to discipline yourself, for it pays big dividends to care for the complexion regularly and consistently—provided, of course, that you use the proper creams and lotions for your particular skin.

Perhaps the best and most effective method of gaining self-discipline is to take a job where you are your own boss. There are many of these positions, and they are easy to get. Here you are put to the supreme test. Say, for instance that you are selling merchandise for general use (these jobs are nearly always selling jobs, and the finest method of gaining poise as well as self-discipline). You must set a certain hour to begin work in the morning, just as definitely as you would if you were going to an office, and stick to it as rigidly as if you were punching a time clock. You must work a certain number of hours a day, every working day. You must keep a certain number of new contacts to be made regularly. You must keep at it week in and week out, just as you would if you were in a factory.

With this program—and by sticking to it—you will overcome the bad habit of procrastination, you will master the bad habit of being without system in your work, you will develop self-assurance, and a certain amount of poise and self-confidence for you will soon find that you are exceedingly proud of your ability to be your own boss. And, probably more interesting, you will find that you are making more money than any regular job in office or factory could possibly pay, for selling jobs, though they are harder, are excellent money-makers for those who master self and systematize their work.

If you have children, whether boys or girls, please do not allow them to grow up without developing this quality. Help them now while they are young. Give them certain little duties about the house, if nothing more than keeping their own rooms, or helping with the dishes, or being systematic in studying their lessons—and impress upon them the importance of being master of self.

You may wonder why I have gone into self-discipline in the discussion of harmony. I have done this because without this quality you cannot overcome the disharmonies which come up. It is impossible to keep your own counsel when Aunt Minnie is absolutely driving you distracted with her constant meddling in your affairs, unless you have disciplined yourself to become master of any situation. There are times when your pride is able to come to your rescue, for when you have mastered this one point, pride of achievement will come to your aid and prevent your being intolerant, or making an unwise remark, or doing something detrimental to your interests.

If nothing else, your training in this can absolutely prevent any arguments and "fusses" with your family and friends. Remember it takes two to make an argument—and you will have mastered yourself to the point where you can remain pleasant and refuse to argue, regardless of the amount of urging on the part of another.

Perhaps the best way to really gain harmony within yourself and your family, friends, and work, is to set about actually disciplining yourself to such a point that you are always master of any situation. This is not only a point gained in the home and office, but it is also a tremendous quality in building a positive, magnetic personality.

CHAPTER 7

Good Sportsmanship

$\mathcal{H}$armony and positive thought have led us to good sportsmanship. Just what is good sportsmanship? Perhaps the best one-word definition of this quality is unselfishness on all occasions.

In the practice of any sport it is essential to remove self from the game in order to be a "good sport." Perhaps one of the best sports in this country is Bobby Jones, the King of Golf. He has yet to criticize an opponent who beat him in a round of golf. He has yet to condemn another man for having gotten the "breaks," or to have considered the weather, the wind, or any one of the thousand things which could have caused him to lose. When Bobby loses a game of golf, he admits he did not play as good a game; the other fellow was better. That is real sportsmanship.

In the game of life—and life is definitely a game—we must be just as good sportsmen as in the game of golf, or bridge, or in any race. Let's do the best that we can, then if we get licked, try harder in the next race and see if we cannot win by merit. Let's not alibi out of it—there is no alibi for failure!

It is well to always bear in mind, "Success requires no apology; failure permits no alibi." This goes for the game of life as well as any sport.

Good sportsmanship requires the development of self-control. Self-control covers so many different points that it needs to be broken down and examined. The word means exactly what it implies, control of self. But how many people have control of self? Very few have complete control of self, and a great number have almost no control over self. Self-control is entirely separate and distinct from self-discipline.

Success requires no apology; failure permits no alibi.

Self-control begins first with the power-house, the moving factor of which is the mind. Do you have control over your mind? Do you think the thoughts you want to think, or are you bothered by petty things bobbing up to annoy you? Do you worry? Do you ever lose your temper? Do you become irritated? If you do any of these things, you do not have control over your mind.

A great many women seem to have the idea that a fit of temper indicates artistic ability or creative genius. A fit of temper definitely points out a person who lacks self-control, one who is subject to moments of complete lack of self-control. When I was a very little girl, I used to display my temper whenever I wanted something. One day, I did this in the presence of my father. He picked me up, sat me on his knee and said very quietly—as if he were ashamed to let me know, "My dear, always remember that a person who is temperamental is 98 percent temper, and 2 percent mental." I was not very good at figures and percentages at the time, but I did recognize just how undesirable that was. From that day on, whenever I began to get "hot under the collar" I just asked myself one question, "Can I get mad and still control myself?" So far, I have been unable to find a way to keep the upper hand while losing my temper—consequently, the temper has been sacrificed entirely to my better judgment.

But how can you get control over your temper? This depends entirely upon how much you desire to get the upper hand. If you really want to master the situation, it would be well to deliberately map out ways and means of going about it. Sit down with yourself and sell yourself the idea that a display of temper brands you a weakling. It makes you a laughing stock, and it places you at the mercy of those about you. You can never hope to be a lady as long as you display a temper. Tell yourself all the terrible things that will come of a sharp and uncontrolled temper. Do this every morning before you begin the day. Be sure you do this before you have a chance to get mad.

By doing this every morning, you will charge your mind to be cautious, and it will begin to make an impression—with time. Do not expect to get up one morning, say a few things to yourself, and immediately find you have control over your temper. Remember, you have been years the servant of your temper, and you must be patient and firm in making it your servant. Servant and master do not change places by mutual consent. The master will fight for his rights, and unless you are persistent, you cannot master your temper.

There is one other thing: You can generally see the fight approaching, as you begin to feel yourself slipping into a state of temper. When you feel this coming, it is best to excuse yourself and leave if possible; if not possible, stick your tongue in your cheek and say nothing until the rage has blown over.

How long will it take? This depends upon two things; first, how sincerely you desire to overcome the trouble, and second, how far you have allowed your temper to go.

In the display of temper, we always talk too much and say things for which we are sorry. But talking too much is not restricted to fits of temper. Talking seems to be an uncontrolled habit with a great many women. It is as though they were regular machines chattering incessantly. It is essential that we talk, but it is neither essential nor desirable that we talk all the time. The women who talk incessantly are women who do not have self-control, they are very poor sports, they generally get mad and fly off the handle when things go against them. Why? Because they have allowed themselves to lose control over self. This may sound farfetched to you, but I assure you it is not.

Most people talk too much anyway. Sometimes we get ourselves into trouble by this constant chattering; we seem to wander off with the rhythm and music of our own voice and leave it there to say whatever it pleases – often it is not very discreet.

If you would take all the conversation the average person participates in for one day, it would be astonishing to learn that so much could be said without anything of importance being mentioned. Good sportsmanship demands a fair exchange of conversation, not a complete monopoly of the floor.

The best way to go about checking up on yourself in regard to how much you talk is to deliberately time yourself for a few days and actually compare the amount of talking you do with that you allow your friends to do. By doing this a few days, you can tell if you are taking too much of the conversation. If you are guilty of this, the best way to restrain yourself is to limit yourself to polite answers for a few days—this will bring you up with a bang. You will realize just how much you were talking. It should cause you to be more conscious of the weakness, and more considerate of your listeners. If the first "silence" does not turn the trick, try it again and again until you have gotten control of your tongue.

Good sportsmanship does not permit arguments. I know a good many people love to argue, and will start one at the drop of the hat. Nine times out of ten, a "friendly argument" leads to bitterness, loss of temper, and often to loss of friends. This is entirely unnecessary, for it takes two to make an argument. If you become a participant, it is your own fault, and you are not displaying the true spirit of sportsmanship, for the odds are too great; there is so much to be lost and nothing to be gained. If you see an argument headed your way, change the subject, for it is impossible to foretell the things that may happen in the heat of an argument.

No doubt the best way to develop good sportsmanship is to follow this simple routine; always give the other fellow the benefit of the doubt, always take the unselfish viewpoint, never claim for yourself any disputed points of advantage, and always play a clean game. Even if you should lose the game, you will win much more in the end by having stamped yourself a better sport. If you have the advantage of the other fellow, do not use this as a means to whip him unfairly. In other words, be unselfish, be fair and just in your dealings with others, do not talk too much, never get into an argument, and above all, never lose your temper.

There is one other thing which good sportsmanship demands—tolerance at all times and in all things. We expect the world and its people to tolerate us; we must, therefore, tolerate the views and opinions of others.

Tolerance, as I refer to it, is directed towards the rights of others. Never would I suggest that anyone tolerate ignorance, illiteracy, poverty, or any other undesirable limitation within one's self!

In the game of life, play the best game you can, play fairly, learn all you can about the game, and tolerate the shortcomings of others. Never play the game with one less experienced than yourself without taking upon yourself the handicaps due an experienced player, otherwise you have broken the first rule of good sportsmanship. Whenever possible, pick a fellow your own size and play a clean game—win, lose, or draw. You will come out richer than you went in, for you will have the respect and admiration of all who know you.

Until you have learned to be tolerant with those who do not always agree with you; until you have cultivated the habit of saying some kind word of those whom you do not admire; until you have formed the habit of looking for good instead of the bad there is in others, you will be neither successful nor happy.

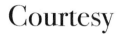

CHAPTER 8

Courtesy

Courtesy is not to be confused with etiquette. Etiquette is purely on the surface, and subject to the whims of fashion, while courtesy originates in—and comes from the heart—and will never change until the human race has changed its nature.

Courtesy is made up of a number of tiny things which may seem entirely unimportant. The strange thing about these little things is they are exceedingly important for they reflect not only a woman's disposition, but the very character and nature of the woman as well as her breeding.

When you realize this, you may become more discriminating in just exactly where courtesy begins. Courtesy, like charity, should begin at home! This may seem a strange place to begin, but as I have said over and over again, every move we make, everything we say, and everything we do is a reflection of our everyday habits. It is easy to see that we must build this particular trait very carefully and diligently, for it may overcome many shortcomings we possess, as well as mark us ladies of the First Order.

Courtesy is made up of four parts; one, the manner in which we do or say a thing; two, tact (which needs no explanation); three, the habit of being democratic; and four, thoughtfulness of others.

These things we recognize and exercise in public. They are the fundamentals of our "company manners" but for everyday use, we seldom consider them important. You ask me why you should be as considerate of your family and immediate friends as you would be of Mrs. Van der Snoot. For the simple reason that at home you are building the habits which you must take out in public. If you build courtesy into your everyday life, it will come naturally and smoothly when you are in public.

Then, too, there are many wonderful dividends paid to those who develop the sincere desire to be thoughtful of others. One of the most outstanding cases of dividends on courtesy was that of a friend of mine.

This young lady became the secretary to a very prominent man. She did not know at the time that he and his wife were near the breaking point, that Reno was just around the corner. But she was sincerely thoughtful and courteous in the extreme. She learned from him just when his wedding anniversary rolled around, his wife's birthday, and various other details. She soon learned that he was in the habit of leaving town without bothering to give his wife any explanation, or even saying where he was going, or when he would be back.

She began to telephone his wife for him to inform her that he had been called out of town on business, and would be away for so many days. Then, when the wire came to the office saying that he would be back, she would phone the wife. In the meantime, she would go out and buy some little article which she thought the wife would like, and when the "boss" showed up, she would hand him the package, and tell him that she was afraid he had not had time to buy his wife a present—this would do, in case he had forgotten. She always ordered flowers when he should send them; she went to the trouble to buy presents (which, of course, she charged to him), for birthdays, anniversary, Christmas, etc., and it was not many moons before he was remembering to do these things for himself again—and the wife was entirely out of the mood for the trip to Reno.

Sometimes, an act of thoughtfulness can undo more damage than all the words of apology in the world. This young secretary was so in the habit of thinking of others, of wanting to do little things for them, that she did not realize she was doing anything out of the ordinary in the little acts of courtesy extended her boss—which may explain to you just how deeply embedded in her heart was the habit of courtesy. Habit is something we cannot take on and off at will.

Once we form a habit—good or bad—we shout to the world just what sort of company we house in our minds.

Let's consider a most conspicuous example of how habit displays itself. It is necessary for a man to open the door for a lady. Some men are clumsy, awkward, and step all over you, make a fuss about it and by this very clumsiness shout to the whole world that if the lady were his wife, he would let her open the door for herself. The man does not realize that he is advertising the fact that he has no manners at home, that he never seats his mother, his wife, or his sister at the table, that he does not display courtesy and good manners as a part of his everyday habits at home.

You have noticed this many times. Of course, you do not tell the man that you know he is not courteous by nature, nor do you indicate that you have noticed his clumsiness—neither will others tell you of your conspicuous efforts to display courtesy in public, but they will be aware of your putting up a "front."

A great many of us seem to entirely overlook the fact that we are creatures of habit. Each and every one of us is a perfect picture of the habits we have built over the years. We build habits through everyday living, not through temporary discipline enforced for special occasions. Accept this as an absolute fact and you will be able to understand the need for being courteous and thoughtful every day to everyone.

Where do we use courtesy in our everyday lives? Where? Among the people we meet in the customary procedure of the day, the servants at home, the subordinates who serve us in the corner store, the boy behind the soda fountain, the taxi driver, the woman who cleans the house, the office boy, the bus driver, the people with whom we associate every day, and most important of all our family! Yes, Mother, Father, little Johnnie, and husband are the most important people in our day, and for that very reason they are the people to whom we should be courteous, and with whom we should be genuinely democratic, tactful, and thoughtful.

Why? Because it is the spirit, the manner in which we deal with our everyday associates which builds us into attractive, magnetic, loveable women; or into crude, tactless, unfriendly souls despised by all. Take this into consideration when you have the urge to snatch your husband baldheaded for not getting to dinner on time, or for having done something for which you wish to upbraid him. Just remember that you are taking from your own personality a loveable quality which you can replace only with great effort and a tremendous amount of self-discipline, self-control, and will-power.

Why should I stress this so strongly? For the simple reason that your actions, your mannerisms, and your thoughts are building habits within you. They leave their mark for good or bad exposed to the eye of the general public. Hard faces with cold eyes need nothing more to bespeak a cold, selfish, domineering woman. A soft sweet smile with a warm look in the eye points out to all a loveable woman who is kind and thoughtful of others—one to whom we are drawn instinctively.

Some people seem to take great pleasure in "impressing" others with their importance and superiority by ordering servants and subordinates about as though they were less than the dust of the earth. They do impress people, but not as they intend—they shout the fact they are ill-bred, inconsiderate, ill-mannered, and undesirable associates.

An outstanding example comes to my mind. It took place in a restaurant in New York not long ago. Several of us were out to dinner and sat at a particular table because of the delightful spirit of the waitress who served that table. We were about as far along as the soup when we heard a man at the next table talking to the same waitress. He told her everything imaginable was wrong with the service. He made himself quite conspicuous by his actions and loud speech. He would show the girl her place! He would tell the manager he was accustomed to decent service! He was above such abuse and treatment! Oh! He was indignant and made no bones about it.

The girl politely apologized for any lack of service and put up no argument. The man left his table in an arrogant manner, sauntering over to the cashier to "get 'em told."

At this moment my hostess called the waitress to the table, saying to her, "Will you please fill my water glass?" She replied courteously and went for the water. When she returned, my hostess said, "You know, I always sit at your table so I will be sure of the best service in town."

The look on that waitress' face, the smile that she displayed indicated that my hostess, by her thoughtfulness, had undone the antagonism of the crude man who had branded himself uncouth and without manners.

Note that he had branded himself, not the waitress! Why? Because he was guilty of the lack of courtesy, the lack of tact, the exceedingly bad habit of considering himself better than his subordinates. He was in no way democratic, and when a person gets "above" being democratic, he reaches the point of being a snob—which is the personification of bad manners, lack of culture, and offensive personality.

Did you ever stop to think of that? It is worth considering the next time you meet the elevator operator or the shoemaker on the street and hesitate to speak.

It is strange, but without exception, you will find a woman (or for that matter a man), of good breeding and culture to be a person of extreme tact and courtesy, and without fail you will find them democratic in the extreme. She will have a warm feeling for everyone, whether prince or pauper. This is very conspicuous by the fact such people are so rare. Good breeding, culture, and refinement cannot be measured by bank balances, street addresses, or social positions!

If you find a woman who is a snob, who tries to show her superiority by abusing those who serve her, you may be sure that you have before you a woman of poor breeding, no culture, and an exceedingly weak character, even though she may tell you of her family tree all the way back to Adam, and try to impress you with Kings and noblemen she knows.

You may also be sure that a person who displays the lack of tact, courtesy and a genuine democratic feeling is suffering from an extreme inferiority complex. This is without fail. Snobbishness is always the outgrowth of a feeling of inferiority. Check up and you will find this to be true.

How can you build courtesy as a habit? I suggest that you start with the people you see most often, and with whom you come in constant contact. The folks at home! This may sound rather radical to you, that I would dare suggest you be courteous to your own husband—you're married to him! Yes! And God pity him if you are not using a bit of diplomacy in your dealings with him. And the children? They would run over you? That's what they are doing now, isn't it? But how do you deal with them? When you come right down to it, aren't they actually guests in your home? Did they pick you as their mother? Did they invite themselves into the world?

Are you not responsible for training them to meet the world on their own some day? How are you training them? Are you training them by setting the example of what you want them to be? Children learn through association and mimicry; habits of thought, of manners, of speech, of courtesy at home. They reflect the things you do, not the things you say for them to do! You may expect them to display—as the product of your training—when they get out in the world away from you, your own habits and mannerisms, thoughtfulness, and courtesies.

Do you realize that you, yourself judge the people you meet by their associates, by their mannerisms, by their speech, and by their behavior in public and particularly in private, if you get close enough to observe?

So are you judged, and so are you judged by your children's habits and manners, for they are only imitating and reflecting your own behavior at home when you are off guard, not when you are displaying company manners.

The sooner we begin to set up a few rules for ourselves in the development of courtesy, tact, thoughtfulness, and democracy as a matter of habit, the better off all of us will be.

It is a good habit to start with the family, with the subordinates with whom you come in contact, by anticipating something good and complimentary to say about them. If you cannot compliment the service or something personal, at least find something good or kind to say about another whom you know in common—or if there is nothing to say, just smile as if you were glad. A little practice in this will begin to form the habit of courtesy.

In the matter of tact, it is well to ask yourself before you speak if you would like that remark said to you. This will cause you to consider the possible effect of a remark before you make it, and save you from blundering.

The best way to form the habit of being democratic is to be on the lookout for familiar faces, and speak to every person you know in a spirit of real friendliness. This should be carefully followed through with those who serve you, and those to whom you do not have to be polite.

Thoughtfulness is developed by deliberately thinking of the other person. Little acts, deeds, kind words, and gestures go to make up thoughtfulness. A card on birthdays, little favors now and then, the personal touch of writing little notes after pleasant visits—there are a thousand and one ways of thinking of the other person which are not costly in money, but pay tremendous dividends in friendships.

Perhaps thoughtfulness of others can do more to overcome short-comings than any other one thing—but it is a strange thing, we cannot develop thoughtfulness without bringing to our personality a certain beautiful quality of sincerity and unselfishness which reflects itself in everything we do.

Courtesy is a science of the highest importance.
It is like grace and beauty in the body, which charm
at first sight, and lead on to further intimacy and friendship.
Courtesy is the oil in the machinery of social life;
it is necessary for comfort, and it helps to make people happy.

CHAPTER 9

Conversation

My y own definition of conversation can be given in very simple language—personal salesmanship. Life is a matter of personal salesmanship. Everything in life is a matter of salesmanship. Every time we converse with anyone, we have an opportunity of selling ourselves as individuals, and upon succeeding in this, we have the opportunity of selling anything we choose, from carpet tacks to marriage.

And speaking of selling marriage, here is a tip to the unmarried woman who would like to attract a husband. There is but one method by which one can do this fairly, and that is by conversation! It is well to bear in mind that every man is looking for an understanding woman—and when he finds one who (through conversation) convinces him she is the one who understands him perfectly, he asks her to marry him!

This is simply a matter of manipulating conversation. There is one rule which is infallible as a starter—every man is most interested in, and prefers to talk about himself, his work, his troubles, his achievements, his ambitions, his ideas, and his views. If you will ask a few leading questions, you can get him to talking about the things which interest him most—and he only asks that you appear interested, sigh occasionally, give an admiring "Oh," or "Ah," now and then, and he will believe you are the most interesting woman in town. If he does not get around to the subject you want to discuss, only a few care-fully designed questions arc necessary, for he is ready and willing to express his views on any subject—and is delighted to find a woman who will not only listen, but who will show interest in and admiration for his wisdom.

Once you have gotten his views, you are free to expound these as your own, knowing full well that they coincide completely with his, and thereby you become a fellow soul, seeking the same things in life, sharing the same views and ambitions.

With this any woman can turn the conversation around to the subject of love and marriage, and before he knows it, he has asked you to marry him; and with practically no effort you have your proposal, and your future husband!

But for the woman who has already found her husband, and who must live in the house with him 365 days a year, salesmanship through conversation is even more necessary if you are to have any peace and happiness in the home. It is a simple matter to land a man, but it is an art to be able to hold him as your lover and sweetheart after you are married to him. This requires salesmanship of the highest order, and conversation with real design and purpose behind it.

> *It is a simple matter to land a man, but it is an art to be able to hold him as your lover and sweetheart after you are married to him.*

In the morning, you must sell your husband on the idea of getting up, then on breakfast, then on getting off to work on time. When he comes home tired and worn out, you must sell him a pleasant evening, or a plate of burned beans, or you must sell him on buying a new refrigerator, or on moving to a better apartment, or on sending daughter to college, or on buying a fur coat—on any one of the thousand and one things which come up in the course of a lifetime. But by definitely planning for the psychological moment and carefully steering the conversation around to the subject, these things can be discussed without antagonism, and with very gratifying results. A half hour of listening to him tell about his own accomplishments will come nearer buying a new car than two weeks of nagging and argument on the subject of a car.

Every business woman should consider herself a saleswoman, whether she is a saleswoman or a stenographer, whether she has a job or is looking for one. Not so long ago, I needed a new secretary and several women were sent to apply for the job. One of them came in and announced she had been sent by So-and-so, and that she understood I was assisting my husband in his work—she knew all about it, for she had read such books of "hooey" before. My husband spent thirty years of research in digging up the information and facts that she so lightly termed "hooey." Do you wonder that she did not get the job? This was purely a matter of salesmanship through conversation, for she was a nice-looking girl, and probably had ability as a secretary, but through the lack of wisdom in conversation, she missed an opportunity to get a good job. Be cautious of what you say when applying for work!

There are times when it is a matter of when to use conversation, and when to refrain from conversation. Sometimes there is nothing we can say to put over an idea. One of the best illustrations I ever saw in this was in an office. A friend of mine was secretary to a man who was very egotistical and hard to handle; he just would not do anything unless he thought it was his own idea. She knew this, and when she decided she wanted new typewriters placed in the office, she did not go to him and request the new machines—she did not mention it to him at all.

She went in and asked him if he would mind if she sent for the repair man to come out and estimate the cost of repairs on the present machines, as the letters were beginning to look bad. Of course, he agreed to an estimate.

Then she phoned the typewriter company, talked with the manager, and told him to send a repair man and their best salesman with a new noiseless machine, and to be sure that they asked for her when they got to the office.

When they came, she placed the salesman with the new machine at a desk which was directly in front of the "boss's" office—where he could easily see all that was going on. She told the repair man to go to work on his estimates of the old machines, and to take his time and make it plenty steep; then she told the salesman to give her a demonstration of the new machine.

In a few minutes, the boss was looking out the door. He came out, sat down at the desk where the new machine was, and began playing with it. The salesman explained all about it, and showed its advantages. The repair man came back with his figures, and they compared the estimate for repairs with the price of new machines.

The boss got the bright idea of putting in new machines throughout the office! Where did he get the idea? Was it his own?

This is an illustration of what to do when it is impossible to sell an idea with conversation. There is a time to talk, and a time to refrain from talking—learn this trick, it will be most valuable in negotiating your way through life, both in business and at home—in landing a husband, and in keeping him.

The clever woman always sells her man an idea by first planting it in his mind as his own, and then lets him sell it to her as his own idea! This is master salesmanship.

There is only one definite rule which will apply to conversation at all times, and under all circumstances; that is for you to remain a lady. This does not allow you the privilege of indulging in some of the popular pastimes of the moment, such as wise-cracking and telling risqué stories—these things are completely out of the question if you wish to sell yourself and make the best impression through conversation.

Wise-cracking has become almost universal through the aid of the motion pictures and radio. If there is one grave danger toward the complete wrecking of a charming personality, it is wise-cracking. It seems that most of the pictures now considered "smart" are strongly tied together with fast moving conversation consisting almost entirely of wise-cracks.

This is all right for paid entertainment, when we wish to get away from the humdrum of life, but many women forget that the very actresses who are so diligently quoting the wit of an author are merely doing so for the purpose of professional entertainment. It is absurd to carry this into everyday life; it is just as ridiculous as it would be for a professional dancer to begin dancing down the street when the natural thing to do is to walk.

You may think it is quite an art to develop a series of smart wise-cracks and spring a new one at every opportunity. But are you so sure it is? Let's see what it will do to your personality, and then you may judge for yourself if it is well to develop this habit.

First, wise-cracks are biting, that is what makes them wise-"cracks," and the moment a woman allows her conversation to become the least bit biting she is on the verge of sarcasm. The moment sarcasm is developed, we find a woman with an exceedingly sharp tongue.

Name the woman with a sharp tongue who has either a pleasing personality or a great many friends. Just name her. Is it so wise to ape the professional entertainers in their efforts to lighten a few moments of an otherwise dull day?

Wise-cracking may be likened to cayenne pepper; in its proper place and in the proper proportions, it makes an otherwise flat dish delightful, but too much above the general run.

The woman who wise-cracks generally tells or listens to risqué stories. Risqué stories, so far as women are concerned, were introduced with Prohibition, which made it "smart" to take a drink. Drink automatically causes a woman to lower her standards of behavior. At this particular time, we shall not go into the evils of drink, we shall concern ourselves with risqué stories. Any woman who tells a risqué story immediately justifies any man in making uncomplimentary advances. This is nothing new. Woman has always set the pace. The wise woman is one who keeps her standards far above the general run.

The wise woman is one who keeps her standards far above the general run.

Women have been given the vote, have been allowed to go into the offices and stores and participate with men on equal footing. She has gained much by this, but unless she is wise and cautious, she will lose much more than she can possibly gain. It used to be that women were extended a great many little courtesies by men, but today the men seem to ignore the average woman insofar as extending favors and showing deference is concerned.

When we consider a group of men and women sitting around for a social evening, the women drinking and laughing at the smutty stories being told, some of them even telling stories at which the others laugh—is that apt to inspire respect and to fascinate men? It cannot, for the simple reason that she has placed herself right on his level, and no man wants to have much to do with a woman whom he cannot look up to. He must place her on a pedestal, even if it is only a tiny one. It is difficult for any man to place a woman on a high level when she even listened willingly to risqué stories, much less when she has actually "swapped yarns."

This has become such a universal pastime that women and girls seem to get a great deal of pleasure in telling these burlesque-house stories among themselves. They will sit and tell them by the hour. I have actually seen some women make notes when they would hear a particularly snappy one. I have heard them say, "Oh, I must tell that to So-and-so, he would love it!" And they take great pride in their ability to remember and tell the stories.

It is very easy to understand just what this does to a woman's personality, when you frankly face the facts. First, I take it for granted that every woman hopes to be thought a lady. Ladies are in no way associated with the vulgar side of life, they remain calmly aloof and sidestep the possibility of being placed in such a position as to even accept vulgarity in their presence. Can any woman be a lady and allow her lips to tell vulgar stories? Can any lady possibly place herself in the same class with the Forty-second Street burlesque women? This is what women do when they tell risqué stories, either to other women or to men.

It is not just what other people think of you that has a bad effect in this respect; the worst part of it all is that you have allowed your mind to fill itself with such filth. Again, I wish to stress the fact that every thought you think and every emotion you have leaves its mark on your face, your heart, and your personality.

However, do not believe I would destroy the sense of humor or discourage the art of laughing heartily. Never! It would be a miserable world without fun, but be sure that your fun is not at the expense of another, that it does you no damage. If your fun must make someone the goat, if you must wise-crack, the least you can do is wise-crack about yourself. If you must tell risqué stories, be sure that you care nothing for the other person's opinion of you, and that you have no right to expect the person to whom you tell the story to hold a very high opinion of you.

But what can I do in conversation? What shall I talk about? What shall you talk about? How could anyone ask that in a world so entirely filled with changing conditions every moment? But there too, you must consider your company. If you were talking with a group of youngsters, you would hardly consider discussing the same topics as you would if you were talking to a group seriously working toward a Ph.D. in some deep subject. The topic selected should first be based upon the interests of the persons gathered, and the scope of their knowledge. This always varies.

If I were talking with Mrs. Jones, whose little Sally had just come down with measles, would she be more interested in my sincere interest in Sally's condition than she would be in the condition of the European situation? On the other hand, if I were talking with a young man who was just preparing to go to Europe for the season, do you think he would be as interested in the measles as he would be in Hitler, Mussolini, Stalin, and the War?

By this ridiculous comparison, I wish to emphasize the necessity of sizing up your prospective conversationalist, and carefully selecting a subject which would be to his interest, and, if possible, of mutual interest. If nothing of mutual interest can be found, then by all means—if you wish to make a good impression—choose something of interest to the other person.

If he is a stranger, and you do not know anything of his likes and dislikes, a few leading questions will inform you. Strange as it may seem, sometimes a good listener who only "Oh's" and "Ah's" now and then is often considered the best conversationalist in the group. Be careful of this. Be sure that the person who is doing the talking is enthralled with the privilege, and that you have not become a dull drag who is incapable of holding up your end of the conversation. There are two extremes against which you must guard: talking too much, and talking too little; either is inexcusable and does irreparable damage to the other person's impression of you.

The art of being a fascinated listener bears more consideration. It is the easiest way out of a tight corner when you find yourself attached to a stranger with whom you have nothing in common, and can find nothing about which you may speak intelligently which will interest him. He may be an archeologist who has just returned from some faraway place. You may hardly know what is archeology, but if you will just lead him on a bit, soon he will open up and entertain you genuinely, and incidentally give you a bit of new knowledge, provided of course, you do not expose your lack of information too quickly.

Speaking of exposing your ignorance, an outstanding instance comes to my mind by way of explanation of this point. It happened when I was in school. If you have ever been to a girl's finishing school, you know that the entire world consists of dances, classes, and the immediate little circle involved. It so happened that I went down to breakfast one Sunday morning (we were allowed to sleep late on Sunday if we chose), and sat down to a nice breakfast. I passed the customary "good morning" to those gathered, and went about the problem of bacon and eggs. I had hardly started before the teacher sitting at the head of the table remarked, "I see the young fellow landed safely in France."

I knew no more of whom she was speaking than if she had been talking a foreign tongue, but being a bit careful of "skinning my ignorance" and knowing the girls so well, I merely smiled and commented, "How fine. Is he all right?"

"Oh, yes," the teacher replied. She had hardly gotten the words out before one of the girls popped out with a barrage of questions. The young lady got a beautiful upbraiding for not having read the papers as she was supposed to do—I got complete information on the subject concerned. The young man in the conversation was none other than Col. Lindbergh on his flight to Paris.

When I feel the urge to say things that will expose my lack of knowledge, or to make a statement of which I am uncertain, I just remember that I almost admitted I was unaware of one of the biggest events in modern history. It is wise to remember that we often learn a great deal by doing only a portion of the talking, and a good bit of the listening. If you are not gifted with the freedom of easy conversation (conversation means the exchange of talk, not an endurance solo), it is best to pick a few topics of general interest and inform yourself on these. I may suggest that operations and your pet complaints are of no interest to anyone except yourself. The only person I know of who would be interested in your ailments is a relative who is waiting for you to die so she can spend your money, and she is interested only if you have money.

Another thing in regard to conversation of utmost importance is the art of showing tolerance for the opinions of others. If you have developed a very rigid set of rules, and are unwilling to deviate or give an inch from these opinions, it is my suggestion that you stay off of controversial subjects, two of which are religion and politics. It seems that labor and capital have joined the list. It is best to handle carefully the subjects in which we find ourselves so deeply involved at this moment of social evolution, sex, drinking, and divorce. These are things which only time will settle. Neither you nor I can begin to speed up nor alter the process of evolution.

Of course, within the range of your interest in an individual, if that person is in need of advice, and you are equipped through your experience with the world to give advice, this is exempted from the classification of conversation and becomes private confidence and counsel. Think twice before you counsel another. Be sure you are right for she may take your advice—and what if it is unsound and unwise?

It is best to force yourself to be tolerant of others. Tolerance has never been a cause for trouble, but the lack of tolerance has fired the first gun in many a battle, both in war and in courts. Tolerance and understanding are so closely related that it is almost impossible to separate them, for if we make it our business to understand, we thereby put ourselves in position to be tolerant.

Perhaps the most common weakness of both men and women in regard to conversation is in that they talk too much. Some women love to hear their voices. They begin chattering when they get up in the morning, and they keep it up all day, just a constant flow of words, words, words with little or no particular meaning. This is a very inexpensive way to entertain one's self, provided you are alone when indulging.

It is surprising just how many things we do tell when we talk too much. The fact is we tell everything we know, be it much or little, and anyone who wants to know anything about us, our family, or our friends can just listen a while and get all the information we have. We seem to overlook this entirely. We seem to overlook the fact that a woman who spends all her time talking, spends none of her time learning, and therefore cannot have much worthwhile knowledge on any subject.

I have a friend who is with one of the large detective agencies. When I asked him some questions about how they get information, he told me that people generally love to hear themselves talk, and if you will just listen a while, throw in a few leading remarks, you will get the information you want. I asked if this was true of the person they were investigating, and he said that sometimes the very person who is being investigated will talk so much that all the information is gained from him direct. And then we say we do not love to hear the sound of our own voices!

I know this is true in business. I know plenty of business men who will not let their wives meet business associates for the simple reason that wives talk too much, and use too little judgment in what they say.

So, if you would become a good conversationalist, avoid the dangers of wise-cracking. Carefully pick your topics to interest those about you. Avoid vulgarity in both choice of words and in the subject matter. Listen a great deal. And above everything else, be tolerant of another's opinion, for that person has been granted the right to freedom of speech and thought in the same document which gives you that privilege—the Constitution of the United States. Surely if our forefathers had such respect for the opinions of every American, we should.

The tone of good conversation is brilliant and natural;
it is neither tedious nor frivolous; it is instructive without pedantry,
gay without tumultuousness, polished without affectation,
gallant without insipidity, waggish without equivocation.

CHAPTER 10

The Voice

In order to illustrate the importance of the voice in our impressions upon others, I shall ask you to consider the dog, a mute creature. If he wants a drink of water he can tell you, not in words, but by the bark. If he wants to get out of the house, he has another bark entirely different from the "water bark." If he wants something to eat, he has still another bark. If there is a stranger prowling around the house, he has a bark that means business. How do you know the difference between these various barks? Because of the various emotions behind the barks.

So it is with geese, with ducks, and with all birds and animals—they have a language of their own, but upon what is it based? Upon intonation of sounds, so far as man has been able to discover.

The human voice is just as clearly based upon the emotions behind the words. No woman can have a colorful, glamorous personality without a voice that is enriched with emotion. Proof of this lies in the effect talking pictures had upon some of our most prominent stars of the silent days.

A great many women seem to have taken it upon themselves to imitate movie stars and others in the limelight, in gesture, in style of haircut, and in manner of speech. I have seen several girls of high school age talking like Greta Garbo. Not that I mean Miss Garbo's voice is wrong; it is the voice that fits Greta Garbo's personality, and any other voice would be a misfit in her. But in some little school girl who is so obviously American, so gloriously young and full of life, a merry, happy voice filled with gaiety is the only possible "fit" for her personality.

The voice, like every other point of personality, must be your own to make you a genuinely individual woman. Of course, if the same things were done in writing, these steals would be plagiarism unless credit were given to the author. If this were possible in regard to women, it would be well, for when you mimic this or that person, you would have to enter a room and announce that you are imitating Miss Hepburn or Miss Lombard, and it would soon put a stop to cheap imitations.

The voice, like every other point of personality, must be your own to make you a genuinely individual woman.

This is particularly obvious in regard to the voice. Your own voice must express your own thoughts, your own emotions, if it is to portray your own personality.

Just as your voice conveys your personality, it conveys your sincerity, your lack of interest, or your intense interest. It shows definitely your self-confidence, your poise or your lack of poise, and your familiarity with the topic being discussed. Remember, I am talking about the tone of voice—not the words. Words convey only thoughts; tone of voice conveys truth or falsehood, sincerity or insincerity, enthusiasm or lack of enthusiasm, interest or lack of interest, knowledge or ignorance of the subject.

By your voice, you may catch and hold the interest of your listeners, or you may fail to catch and hold their interest. This is done by your ability to color your voice, by the knack of emphasizing just the right words in order to convey the exact meaning. You may say "how-do-you-do," and never make an impression, or "how-do-you-do" and make a wonderful impression, or you may swallow the whole thing and be a complete loss, "howd'y'do." There is a vast difference!

The most practical and applicable information I have found on the development of the voice for the non-professional is a book called *Personal Magnetism*, by Shaftsbury, Ralston Society, Meriden, Conn. This book has a chapter on the voice which has been recommended by many voice teachers, and is not a very lengthy chapter.

Women should have their voices placed by someone who knows how. This can be done in a few lessons, and at nominal expense. It is a good idea to be certain that you do not talk through your nose in a high-pitched scream. The whine is probably the most offensive of all voices—it seems to get on the nerves and is most irritating. By that very fact, it destroys the personality and is totally without charm and color.

Perhaps the best way to check on yourself is to have a record of your voice made. There are thousands of inexpensive recording places scattered all over the country where you can make a record for a few cents.

Another important factor to be considered is the volume or the loudness with which you speak. For the average woman it is not necessary to "raise the voice" to be heard. There are two dangers if one raises the voice—one goes to a higher pitch which is less alluring, and one naturally puts behind a higher pitch more "steam," and actually becomes louder. This does two things, it indicates lack of culture, and also lack of consideration for those around you. It may center attention upon you for the moment, but it is not favorable attention—be sure of that.

I warn those who live around people who are hard of hearing and have developed the habit of shouting for their benefit, this is entirely unnecessary if you will develop the habit of slowness and clearness of lip movement. I know this from experience, and I also know it from teachers of speech to the deaf. It is not the volume which counts as much as it is the clarity with which you speak.

Perhaps if I bring to your attention the most outstanding voice on the radio, you will understand what I mean by clarity and tempo. President Roosevelt, unquestionably, has the most outstanding radio voice in the country. This is acknowledged by experts. The next time he speaks, if you will sit down and study his method of speech, you will understand just why he is the outstanding radio personality.

His voice is cultivated, soft, modulated, smoothly flowing; his intonations are most dramatic, and his tempo is far from that of the commercial announcer who is trying to say as many words as possible in as little time as possible, because his sponsor has forced him to do so. No! The President is not so concerned with the number of words he speaks as he is with the understanding of those words you will grasp; therefore, he says fewer words in the time allotted than does an announcer whose sponsor has no knowledge of the tempo of the voice.

On the other hand, extreme enthusiasm and excitement are conveyed by a faster tempo. A more staccato rhythm such as Graham McNamee uses in describing a football game. In this instance, color, speed, suspense, and enthusiasm are portrayed by the tone and the swift-ness of the speech.

Tempo is something that must be understood to be appreciated. It is not just the slowness, it is also speed—but the proper tempo is not a monotonous humdrum of slowly pronounced words on one note. The proper tempo of the voice is the speed with which your thoughts can be picked up by the listener. This is always the pace to be set by the speaker. Remember, you are only the speaker, you know what you are saying. The other fellow is the listener, and must catch what you are saying. This is the most important point in tempo.

The most perfect speaker I know is a teacher of speech. In fact, she teaches speech to the totally deaf. She is not an American-born woman, and one would naturally expect her to have her native accent, but I defy anyone to discover her nationality by her speech. It is clear, perfectly enunciated, the inflection (the variations of volume, pitch, and coloring of the voice) are entirely individual and beyond reproach. She has developed the art as a profession.

If you are a southerner, you bear all the earmarks of a southerner, and consequently speak with the southern accent. To alter this would be to destroy a part of yourself. Speak good English, go to the trouble to have your voice placed, attempt to color your conversation with inflections and enthusiasm, but to destroy your accent would be to destroy your individuality. This is true only because you happen to have the earmarks of the South, not only in speech, but in thought, etiquette, and personal mannerisms, as well as in personality. It is difficult to eliminate physical and social heredity. These things are given us and we are bound by them until such time as we become strong enough to eliminate or to alter them.

If you are a French woman, speak with a French accent; it does you no harm, and it harmonizes with your personality. If you are a New Englander, speak with a New England accent; offer no apologies for this is a part of you. But be sure that you are understandable, and that you speak for the other person's benefit, not just for your own pleasure.

Proof of just what may be accomplished in the development of the voice lies perhaps most dramatically in Mrs. Roosevelt. Do you remember when she first began to speak on the radio? She had a most annoying voice; there is no question of this. Every radio critic mentioned it at the time. But what has happened? As she realized that her voice had to be adjusted to the radio, she began to train it. Now, when you hear Mrs. Roosevelt, you hear a rich, full, colorful voice. It is the same woman, the same individuality; she has lost none of her personality, but has cultivated a more pleasing voice—those high-pitched, rasping sounds are gone.

How did she do this? By development! She corrected little things which she did not recognize without the cold impartiality of radio. This is something for all of us to consider, for radio is definitely a career for women today—and will become even more so in the future.

If I have dwelt too long on the professional development of the voice, may I mention the fact that the best measuring stick of anything is its commercial value? Perhaps this can be best demonstrated by two young women who have exceptional records in their voices. One has devoted her life to the cultivation of her voice, the other has had little or no professional training. These two are Grace Moore and Kate Smith. Grace Moore has one of the most glorious cultivated voices of our day, while Kate Smith has an uncultivated voice of richness and color that comes straight from her heart. It is not Kate Smith's voice that we applaud, it is Kate Smith herself.

In the case of Miss Moore, we do not concern ourselves with Grace Moore, the woman, for we are so enchanted with the perfection of her marvelous voice. You may be able to understand what I mean by the importance of the voice in everyday conversation, just as you can tell by the way in which a person speaks if there is distress, happiness, extreme excitement, or just plain "hello" at stake. One seldom announces a fire in the same tone of voice and with the same emotion that one announces dinner.

How often you are irresistibly drawn to a plain, unassuming woman, whose soft silvery tones render her positively attractive! In the social circles, how pleasant it is to hear a woman talk in that low key which always characterizes the true lady; in the sanctuary of home, how such a voice soothes the fretful child and cheers the weary husband.

CHAPTER 11

Showmanship

*S*howmanship is, simply speaking, the art of dramatizing the commonplace, of glorifying the ordinary things of life, the ability to attract favorable attention to one's self by design—and at will. This is just as necessary to the individual woman as it is to the professional actress, the extreme to which she should go is limited to her "public." The only reason that an actress needs a publicity man, and must dramatize herself before great numbers of people is because her income and her success depend entirely upon the box office, which is supported by the public.

You and I need no publicity man, we need no public ballyhoo. You and I are just everyday women living simply within the range of our incomes, and have to concern ourselves with the butcher, the baker, and the candlestick maker. There are many little things which make up our everyday lives, but a good impression on the people with whom we come into contact, and particularly those with whom we must live, is just as advantageous to us as a good impression on the public is to an actress. It is a known fact that before any woman can attract the right man, she must make herself attractive in speech, clothes, manners, and in every action so that it will bring favorable attention. This is showmanship.

The chances are we seldom realize that it is carefully developed show-manship which enables Peggy Hopkins Joyce to attract men of means to her. She has married many, and all of them exceedingly wealthy. This is showmanship on her part, carefully planned and carried out to the desired end.

It is just as necessary that a young girl use showmanship in attracting young men on the dance floor—if she is to be sure of a good "rush." I learned this trick many years ago, when I was in school and going to a great many dances. I found a brilliant crescent comb which served as an attention-getter on the dance floor. The other girls could not figure out why I got a better "rush" than they. The answer was simple: With this particular shiny object placed in my hair (which is very dark), I made it easy for the boys to find me. This was nothing more nor less than showmanship, even though I did not realize it at the time. I just knew that when I wore the object I had a better time than when I did not wear it.

In business, showmanship is necessary. One of the cleverest bits of showmanship on the part of a woman in business of which I have ever heard is that which is told of Martha Berry, the woman who has built a school in North Georgia for mountain boys and girls. Miss Berry needed a million dollars for the expansion of her school. She picked Henry Ford as the man to give the money. When she first approached Mr. Ford, it is said that he was entirely disinterested, and refused to give her the money. But Miss Berry asked him if he would contribute a sack of peanuts—a very small donation. Mr. Ford complied.

The next year, Miss Berry came back with five hundred dollars, which she presented to Mr. Ford, explaining that her boys at school had planted Mr. Ford's peanuts, raised a crop and marketed it, and this represented his investment of the year before. Mr. Ford became interested in Miss Berry's project, stopped by and took a look, donated the money she needed, and continued to take an interest in what she was doing. Even today he goes by and spends time with the boys and girls in Miss Berry's school, and has given them many things of value—just as the result of Martha Berry's ability to dramatize something as prosaic as a common peanut! If the peanut can be turned into a million dollars through showmanship, who knows what we may do with ourselves? There are opportunities on every side.

Just how does one go about dramatizing the ordinary? Perhaps the best illustration is right in the theatre where showmanship is the life— or the death—of a production. Have you ever been behind the scenes in a theatre or in a picture studio? It would give you some idea of just how much can be done in your own mind through make-believe. It is wonderful just how effectively and how remarkably well these people live in the land of make-believe. On the set of a picture production, one will find stage settings which are so obviously makeshift and artificial that it would be ridiculous to imagine anyone accepting them as real. There are countless technicians, cameramen, directors, and a mere handful of actors. These actors go through the same scene, not once, but dozens of times. They are real people, even as you and I; they have their ups and downs, they have their personal problems and lives just as we do. But for the moment they remove themselves and become puppets at the command of the plot of the play.

A real he-man may be standing there with powder and paint on his face, making him look so ridiculous as to be laughable, but for the effect of the finished picture he must bear these things. He is not thinking of how he looks, of how silly he may appear standing there under more powder and cosmetics than any woman would dare use. He is living the part of another man built by the author, to follow through to a certain end.

This we seem to admit to ourselves, but we always add, "Think of the money he makes, think of his fame, think of the marvelous home he has. I would be willing to put up with that for what he gets out of it." Or, in the case of an actress, we remark, "She is so beautiful, she spends a fortune on clothes, she has everything, and she doesn't have to wash dishes and tend to the children. I could do it too, with her breaks."

This is not a book on success in business. Those rules have been set down and are available to all. This is intended to help you in your own little world to learn to live and to make your life fuller and happier.

How can you dramatize yourself? I may state right now that making a clown of yourself is not effective showmanship! Like everything else, there is a happy medium, and there is a point beyond which we must not go.

Not so long ago, I was walking down Fifth Avenue in New York, and just as I crossed the street I saw a little dog sitting on his hind legs, his front legs held out in obvious astonishment. The dog was on a leash and he refused to move when his mistress started to cross the street. He just sat and stared. You could almost hear him saying, "Do you see what I see?" The lady looked down the side street where the dog was staring, I looked, and several others stopped and looked. We were fascinated by the dog's action, by the expression on his face, but when we saw a well-dressed woman leading a goose up the street, we felt as completely astonished as the dog. The goose had on a big red checkered apron, a red collar, and to that was attached a leash.

Now I admit the goose-woman was dramatizing herself, but I seriously doubt if the effect was just what could be termed desirable. There is a limit beyond which you must not go.

You say that you have a very prosaic circle of friends. That is fine, for it is much easier to dominate the prosaic group than the colorful. In any group, your ability to dramatize yourself hinges on the degree to which you have developed your conversational ability, the color of your voice, and the thought-habits with which you live, plus one other thing—your physical appearance.

Physical appearance is apt to be interpreted as "good looks," or "beauty." How wrong that is! How very wrong! Physical attraction does not lie within beauty, for so exceedingly few can be termed beautiful, and even that is a matter of opinion. The measuring stick of beauty rests too heavily upon the social heritage of man.

It is well for us to study ourselves from the physical side as to type. Are you a baby-face? One to wear ruffles and become a charming but very clinging vine? These are exceedingly attractive when they are natural.

Are you the willowy type? This type generally wears extreme styles most successfully, and bears an air of sophistication. These women are charming—if they are themselves!

Are you the business type who wears very tailored clothes and does everything with efficiency? These are truly a god-send.

Pick your type, study your good points, and devise ways and means of displaying your good points. Then study your weak points and find ways and means of strengthening these, if possible. Make them less conspicuous by overshadowing them with your good points.

But there is something which a great many women seem to overlook entirely, that is the personality of the house in which they live.

If you can control the apartment or the house, the physical setting of the entire place can be built around your own personality just as carefully as your own clothes are built around your personality. But for those who do not control the entire house it is rather difficult. The best way of doing this is to select carefully the people with whom you live, making sure they are agreeable, and of the same general type as yourself.

If you must live with certain people, then it is best to sit down and consider yourself in relation to them. Analyze them, see if you and they are in harmony. If they are pessimistic and always in the dumps, it is time for you to begin working on their minds, for no one can live in gloom and have a charming personality. No house is fine enough or beautiful enough to overcome the thoughts of the people who live within its walls.

If you cannot control the physical setting, you may inject personality in the home by attempting to clean up the thoughts of those who live with you. There are some houses which make you feel uncomfortable, for you could not sing or whistle within their walls if you tried. There are other houses where there is a gay and happy feeling, you are happy to be there, and the day is better for your having come within those walls. The difference between these houses is not the money they cost, not the location or the physical appearance of the houses; it is the thoughts of the people who dominate the house. Show me a house and I can tell you by the way I feel when I enter it if I would like its inhabitants.

There are many little things which can be done to help the physical appearance of the house, little personal touches that make an otherwise drab room more colorful. Just as you may take a very plain tomato, a leaf of lettuce, and a spoonful of mayonnaise and have an unappetizing salad, so you may take the same tomato, the same leaf of lettuce, and the mayonnaise and with a few twists of the wrist, a dash of paprika and have a treat fit for a king. So it is with life, it is just the twist of the wrist that makes a very prosaic tomato into a delightful delicacy tempting to the dullest appetite. That twist of the wrist is called showmanship.

If you would develop showmanship, begin by examining yourself as to type, then search for your good points, accentuate these. Next, take inventory of your weak points, and seriously set about correcting them as far as possible, never accentuating them but always burying them under your good points. Last, but not least, develop your imagination; learn the art of make-believe in turning the commonplace into fairyland.

Remember that the qualities of the heart and the actions of life stamp the features with an ineffaceable mark, either with goodness or vileness; cultivate those affections and habits which will write upon your countenance that which no one reading can but love and admire.

CHAPTER 12

Personal Appearance

*W*hen we think of personal appearance, we generally begin with clothes, then beauty shops, then the figure. But do we think of these in their relative position to our own personality—to ourselves? The relationship of personal adornment to self is of the utmost importance, for it is here that we must distinguish between fashion and personality.

If tiny hats cocked over one eye are the fashion, and you happen to be the dignified type, should you follow fashion or adjust fashion to your personality? Many women say quickly and without hesitation, "Take the hat that is in style." But let's go into that a bit further. A hat that does not suit your own individuality is never becoming, and being unattractive on you, it cannot be fashionable on you. Always bear this in mind when selecting clothes.

You may envy some women for the wonderful clothes they wear, but are you envying the clothes, or their wisdom in selecting the clothes? Just stop and think! I have already touched upon this point rather fully in a previous chapter, and I may add, it is not the amount of money that is spent on clothes that makes the woman; rather, it is the care with which they are selected to suit the wearer which makes the clothes.

It is not the amount of money that is spent on clothes that makes the woman; rather it is the care with which they are selected to suit the wearer which makes the clothes.

To illustrate my point, I shall give two examples within my own acquaintance. One is a very wealthy woman who spends a most astounding sum of money for her wardrobe each year. She has furs that are unbelievably soft and luxurious and jewelry that is insured at a terrific figure, yet she looks like a walking billboard of what not to wear. Her clothes do not suit her type nor her size. They do not set off any of her good qualities (and she has many), but they emphasize all the bad points. The very fact that she is trying to impress everyone with the amount of money she spends on clothes screams out obviously.

I know another woman who has little money to spend, and has very few clothes, but she is known as the best dressed woman in her circle. Why? Because she selects every item of her wardrobe with the utmost care. She is sure that everything suits her individuality; that she is not accentuating her bad points—which happens to be feet that are too large. She wears inconspicuous shoes, and by this I do not mean drab shoes. The shoes fit into the color scheme and theme of the entire ensemble, thus one loses sight of her feet. She keeps her clothes always immaculately clean and neat, and sees that her accessories are interchangeable, for she cannot afford many things. The things she does have become a perfect setting for her own personality, which incidentally is quite genuinely sincere and delightful.

It may be well to mention the fact that the woman who spends so much money on her clothes sets off exactly that same personality, one of veneer with nothing to back it up—money and no background. Strange, isn't it, how we advertise to the world exactly what we are in everything we do.

The actual buying of clothes ranges so widely that it is impossible to give an estimate of how much one should spend on clothes. This has to be adjusted to income and station. Colors, styles, and what-to-have is so entirely dependent upon the mode of living that it is impossible to set a guide. One who makes her living in formal evening gowns would be foolish to buy business dresses. One who makes her living in an office would be foolish to have a dozen house dresses. While for the woman who lives at home, these would be more useful than either of the other wardrobes.

You may say this is ridiculous—why even suggest such unreasonable selections! Why? Because it is not so much the clothes one wears as it is the appropriateness of the clothing that counts. Once when I was a girl, I went on a moonlight picnic, an old-fashioned hayride. On these occasions we rambled about through the woods, and generally climbed a mountain. One girl on this particular hayride was dressed in a dinner gown—a beautiful thing—and silver slippers. Lovely clothes, but they were out of place; we were going to the country, not to a dinner.

There are many offices and stores that have, in recent years, set up restrictions on what their clerks and stenographers may wear. Why? Simply because of the poor judgment on the part of the women themselves. This is true in every walk of life, not just in business.

Just as this is true in clothing, so is it true in the make-up and the hairdress. Most women now go to professionals for hairdressing. This is a wise move, for few women can handle their own hair quite as well as a professional hairdresser. In this, I cannot go too far to stress the importance of neatness. If a woman's hair, nails, feet, and face are in good order and well groomed, she can make a good appearance.

The beauty parlor has become quite a problem to women. I know, for I have had to travel, to shop around, to have my hair botched up, and cut the wrong way; but where a woman lives in the same place most of the time, it is quite easy to find a satisfactory operator. Search around until you find the barber who seems to be able to cut and dress your hair to best advantage, then stick with him. This will benefit you in many ways. First, it will give you a feeling of security in the service; second, it will give you a "stand-in" with the beauty parlor, which comes in mighty handy on special occasions when you must get a little rush service.

If you go to an efficient hairdresser who knows his business, generally he knows better about how your hair should be cut than you do, and also about how it should be dressed. This is particularly important today with so many different extreme styles circulating; we must first see if they "fit the type," and this can be best judged as a rule by another, and by a trained eye.

I have found that the regularity of beauty parlor visits has a lot to do with the results. For general upkeep, once a week is good enough to keep in fair trim. By this, I mean shampoo, hair trim, wave, and manicure. Of course, if anything of importance comes up between times, when it is necessary and to your advantage to be well groomed, it is best to drop in the beauty parlor and have things touched up.

At first you may begrudge the money spent in the beauty parlor. If you have not developed the habit, about three weekly visits to a satisfactory place will convince you that it does something to your personality that is well worth the investment. I may add for the woman in business, it is absolutely essential. For the unmarried woman who is seeking a husband, personal appearance and perfect grooming are of the utmost importance. For the married woman who wishes to keep her husband, it is even more important.

There is only one warning to be given in regard to this, that is over-doing the thing. There are many women who attempt to make of themselves raving beauties by a trip to the beauty parlor. They force the operators to "give them the works," and they come out abso-lute atrocities! False eyelashes, false eyebrows, or false anything else must be done only by the most expert hand and with exceeding caution; otherwise they become horrors, and completely destroy the end desired. These extremes must be avoided by the average woman.

Dying or bleaching the hair is another thing for an expert, and not for an amateur. Be sure before you bleach or dye your hair that you are in the hands of an expert; also that you have the money to maintain it for it needs touching up astonishingly often. Hair that looks artificial seldom improves the looks of any woman.

It is best to understand there is a basic fundamental of personal appearance: neatness. Without neatness, all the beauty parlors in the world cannot make a pretty woman of you, nor can the finest clothes in the world make you attractive.

Neatness is a habit, and one that is conducive to good health, for cleanliness of body and clothing are essentially a part of good health.

There are other details which must be attended to, such as super-fluous hair under the arms and on the shins. The remedies for this are numerous and simple. I, personally, prefer a safety razor. You may prefer some depilatory, but be sure that this is kept neat even when you are wearing long sleeved dresses, for this hair accumulates perspiration odors and becomes offensive, not to mention the actual damage that it can do to clothes. If you perspire freely, I suggest a deodorant. There are many on the market which are thoroughly reliable and very effective. This, too, is essential, as body odors are most annoying.

At this point it is wise to mention the thing that bothers women most—"that time of the month" when it is so exceedingly difficult to cope with the situation. Body odors just seem to accumulate in spite of anything and everything we do. This is entirely unnecessary. Be more punctilious about your precautions in the way of deodorants and cleanliness of the body at this time than usual. Change your pad at least three times during the day, and more often if you have trouble. This will help more than anything else.

There is another important thing to be looked after at this time more carefully than ordinarily—your underwear. This should be fresh every day, but at this particular time, be sure that you are wearing fresh underclothes every morning, and if you go out in the evening, make a complete change. This will make a tremendous difference, for it is astonishing how many odors cling to underwear.

But back to normal care of neatness. We find ourselves confronted, particularly in hot weather, with a foot problem, whether it be corns, bunions, or just plain hot feet that perspire too freely. I have found a way of taking care of the feet that has proven entirely satisfactory for me, and I feel sure it will be of help to you.

First, of course, I must take for granted that your shoes are properly fitted. No woman can possibly have good posture or hope to be poised if she wears ill-fitted shoes that pinch and hurt. Second, it is absolutely imperative that the feet be washed every night. Third, it is just as essential that you never put on a pair of hose that are not freshly laundered.

Granting that the shoes fit, that you keep your feet clean, and wear clean hose, I shall offer a simple care of the feet which are not suffering from corns. When you bathe, soak your feet a little longer than usual, or just soak the feet in hot water for about five or ten minutes, then rinse with cold water, dry them and massage them thoroughly with a generous portion of lotion. Massage the bottoms of the feet, for that is where you stand. Massage them until the skin absorbs the lotion entirely. Do not leave the feet damp or sticky. It is comforting to either dust a little powder over the feet after the treatment, or to use a little powder in the shoes. Never wear a pair of hose more than one time without washing them. This is exceedingly important, both for the health of the feet and the life of the hose.

If you have foot trouble, corns, etc., it is my suggestion that you do not attempt to cut the corns. Use a good corn plaster, and if this does not turn the trick, then call on the chiropodist. For women who have already ruined their feet with ill-fitted shoes, I suggest regular calls on the chiropodist until your feet are back in good condition.

The bath and the foot massage should become everyday routine. The nails usually need a little in-between touching up. A good manicure once a week, with the touching up of polish along as you need it should keep the nails in fair shape. But, be careful of the polish you select. Unless you have beautiful hands and shapely nails, go easy on the brilliant polishes. It is unwise to attract attention to something that is not very pretty. Short boxy nails should be neat, but inconspicuously polished. Rough hands should be equally neat, but inconspicuously polished. Soft white hands with beautifully shaped nails may be polished with even the most brilliant hue and still be exquisite.

The care of the hands and nails beyond the manicure is something which can produce astounding results. Of course it goes without saying that the hands should be massaged with a good lotion every time they are taken out of water. If the hands are particularly rough and red, use an olive oil bath for the hands about once a week, until the condition is corrected. This will not only put the skin back in shape, but it will also give the nails new life. Even though neither the nails nor hands seem bad enough for the olive oil bath once a week, it is not a bad idea to soak the nails in olive oil once in a while, just to keep them from becoming brittle and to stop hangnails.

The eyebrows should be checked over about once a week, just to be sure that they do not lose their neatness, and I may suggest that you follow the natural line of the brow when plucking them. Do not try to reshape them, for this is practically impossible without showing the old line. Nature has placed a definite line there which was designed as a part of your face; keep the brows neat, but stick to the natural line!

The elbows are another problem which often give us trouble. If they are the least bit bony, they have an appearance of being dirty.

The rind of half a lemon rubbed on the elbows about once a week, and lotion rubbed on the elbow after the daily bath will do wonders toward whitening them up.

The hair should be washed at home once in a while and dried in the sun with generous brushing. It used to be that women took much better care of the hair when they wore long hair, for it was necessary to brush it nightly and to take good care of it. But today, we merely wash it, plaster it down, and sit under the dryer until it dries; then we try to muss it as little as possible. This may be good for the wave and the "set," but not for the hair. If it is possible for you to do so, the day before you go to the beauty parlor for a "set," give your hair a good stiff brushing, a shampoo, and dry the hair in the sun. After all, the hair needs a chance to exercise once in a while. It is rather hard to find a beauty operator who will give the hair a good brushing and massage it dry.

We have led up to what is probably the biggest problem in the whole of personal appearance, the care of the complexion. We all realize full well that the skin must be cared for or we become old too soon, and find it impossible to look our best. But since the coming into use of cosmetics, the market has been flooded with everything imaginable—some unhealthy for the skin. When all advertisers promise the bloom of youth, wedding bells, fortunes, and popularity with the use of their products, how are we to know what to use?

We have recognized the fact that we must not trust our own judgment when buying eyeglasses, or in filling the teeth, or in prescribing our own medicines. We even go to a specialist when our feet need treatment, to a specialist to have the hair dressed, but most women use their own judgment in the care of the skin and the selection of cosmetics.

There are a few exclusive shops where specialized individual service can be had, but these are so far beyond the average pocketbook that few can patronize them. The present situation caused me to look about for someone who had made a study of the complexion and of cosmetics, in order that I might pass on to you something practical and useful. I found a man who has devoted fifteen years to personalized cosmetic service. He emphasized the fact that many women buy their cosmetics by the appearance of the package, knowing nothing of the qualities of the contents, and never stopping to consider whether or not the product is suited to the individual skin. I blushed when he said this, for I remembered having bought a box of powder not so long ago because I liked the box it was in.

However, he stated that the average modern woman is anxious to know more about the care of the complexion, and has the intelligence and common sense to consider the benefit to be derived from the use of a preparation. She wants to know what to use, and how to use it.

There are two types of preparations: those for the purpose of keeping the skin, and those to improve the appearance. The first type, for the purpose of keeping the skin, must be selected with regard to the condition of the skin—and if there is any skin disease or trouble, no woman should try to buy cosmetics for treatment. Then, too, the age of the woman must be considered in the selection of these preparations. A woman of twenty would use an entirely different preparation than would a woman of forty.

The second type, or the make-up preparations, should be selected with regard to the natural coloring of the complexion, the eyes, and hair.

For a general procedure, which most women should follow in the care of the complexion, at night a thorough cleansing and careful application of a lubricating cream. In the morning, apply a skin refreshener (or if you prefer, rinse the face), apply a protective base, then the make-up. In the use of make-up, apply just enough to give a natural look—a painted or artificial face is never attractive. Bear this in mind when applying rouge, lipstick, and particularly in the use of eye-shadow. Be careful that you select the most becoming shade of powder and rouge.

This brings to mind the pointers to be considered in the selection of cosmetics, for a great deal must be taken into consideration before an article is selected for your skin. The chief concern should be the condition of the skin before make-up is applied. The question of general health is important; a woman in poor health with a faulty skin should consult a doctor, not a clerk behind the counter who knows no more about the skin or what it needs than she does about Einstein's theory. Cosmetics should be selected with regard to the condition of the skin, not offered as a treatment or a cure for the condition.

When one is young and healthy, there is a freshness and loveliness about the complexion which begins to fade as we grow older. Granting that one has a healthy skin, a simple routine of keeping it every day will prevent a woman from fading as quickly as if the complexion is not cared for. This period of fading generally creeps up on us around the age of thirty, and from that point on the skin ages more rapidly. All women over thirty should be particularly persistent in the daily care of their skin.

As to the proper methods of massage, the movements to use, these are so generally known it seems almost unnecessary to go into detail— and too, most every jar of cream carries with it a chart of instructions on the proper movements for a good massage. There is one thing to remember—always keep the movements upward and outward.

May I remind you again, now that we have gone into the how's and why's of keeping yourself perfectly groomed, and of how to take care of your complexion—there is no jar of cream on the market that will make as good an improvement as a general house-cleaning of your own mind. Lines show in the face, but they come from the mind—remember that when you try to iron them out with creams and lotions!

Lines show in the face, but they come from the mind.

A taste for beauty is worthy of being cultivated;
man dwells with felicity on ideal female attributes,
and in imagination discovers beauties and perfections
which solace his wearied hours, far beyond any
other resource within the scope of human life;
it, cannot, therefore, be unwise to cultivate and
refine this natural tendency, and to enhance,
if possible, these charms of life.

PART THREE

How a Woman "Wins Her Man"

CHAPTER 13

To Marry or Not to Marry

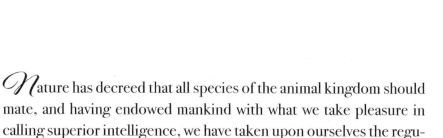

*N*ature has decreed that all species of the animal kingdom should mate, and having endowed mankind with what we take pleasure in calling superior intelligence, we have taken upon ourselves the regulation of mating. We have set up rules which have altered with the changing of time, and have reached a state of chaos in our modern civilization.

Every human being needs someone to love, for life without love is a barren existence. The most complete life in the world for the average woman is that which is built around her husband, whom she loves dearly, and the children of their union.

But so many women use bad judgment in selecting a husband, or even worse, no judgment at all. In recent years, since divorce has become more of a game than a disgrace, the plunge into the sea of matrimony is too often made with the thorough understanding, "If it doesn't work, we'll quit." Any woman who takes the step into marriage lightly is headed for trouble. There are so many things that can happen to leave open wounds and ugly scars upon the heart and the personality of the woman who unwisely selects a husband!

The custom was, in the days of old, for the parents to arrange the wedding, selecting the groom, and the girl was left no alternative.

But with the emancipation of woman came the privilege of selecting for herself the man she prefers as a life partner. Marriage should be anticipated with all the seriousness of the clause, "until death do us part," for without this feeling of permanence, marriage can never bring the fullest enjoyment of happiness and a well-rounded life.

But how does one go about selecting a husband? All men are alike. Ah! but you are wrong. All men are not alike, at home and at heart. There is a very definite plan for selecting a husband.

First, you must study yourself very closely, know exactly what you want of the future, and what type of man would fit into your scheme of things. If you are a woman who loves the little village in which you live, and would be miserable living in some distant place, you would be foolish to marry a man whose dreams carried him beyond the village boundary. Take a local boy who will always be content to stay in the little town and earn a good living for you and your children.

If you are a gypsy at heart, loving to roam, desiring to see the world, it would be equally ridiculous to marry a man who was a home-body, content and happy only in his own community with his family and friends.

If you are a career woman, be doubly cautious as to the man you marry. Be sure that he understands you intend to go ahead with your career, and be positive that he is willing to subordinate himself to you and to live in your reflected glory. This is exceedingly hard for any man, for a man likes to believe himself head of the house and the dominant factor. Any career woman must move cautiously when contemplating marriage. You have only to look about to see how many have hit the rocks, perhaps through no fault of their own.

No woman should marry any man she doesn't admire and respect. No woman should marry a man with whom she has nothing in common. There must be a common meeting ground before there can be a satisfactory marriage. No woman should marry a man who is not a pal and a companion. No woman should marry without a complete and thorough understanding of finances, business, future plans, and household arrangements–including in-laws.

People refuse to buy an automobile without knowing its capabilities, cost, upkeep expense, and lasting qualities, yet they march down the aisle with a pair of pretty blue eyes and stake the rest of their lives on what is behind those pretty blue eyes–sometimes it is a cad, sometimes a god–but it is best to know before the journey to the altar.

Every woman who is not married and who is not in love with her work should be definitely searching for her man. She should know so well what she wants that she can recognize him, for there is "her man" for every woman.

It is well to develop a sort of measuring stick for yourself with which to judge the men you meet. The first rule to be set down, and perhaps the only one of importance, is to keep on searching until you find exactly the man you are looking for. "Oh," you say, "but I would be an old maid." Well and good, better to be a happy old maid than an unhappily married woman when you meet the man of your dreams. And, if you keep on looking, you will find him–provided you know exactly what you are looking for.

It is foolish for a woman to think for a second that she is an old maid and unfortunate if she is not married at an early age, or for that matter, if she never marries–provided she has something to do with herself and her life. Time was not so many years ago, when woman could do little except serve as chief cook and bottle-washer to some married sister if she did not have a husband of her own. Those days are gone forever.

It used to be that girls felt they must get married before they reached the age of twenty-five, whether they were in love or not—they just had to get married. Why, nobody has been able to give a plausible reason.

There are many things which women seek in marriage. Some women are entirely uninterested in happiness, home, and peace of mind, but are interested in social advantages. It may be all right, but I have always thought it rather an underhanded way to climb the social ladder, through marriage entered into for that purpose, though it is generally a sure and very secure way. If this is what you are seeking, be sure that you are not going to throw a jealous fit when your husband finds and becomes interested in someone else, for he will. You cannot give him the little end of a bargain and expect him to remain a mere puppet on a string. After all, he is a man with a mind of his own, and a desire for love and affection from a woman, and if he does not get it from his wife, the world is full of women.

There are some women who marry for money. These generally figure out the alimony possibilities within their own minds before marriage. They are incapable of being hurt, they are merely coaxing their prospective husbands to play at a crooked gambling table.

We are all paid in full measure for the things we give in life. They always end up bitter, hardened, unattractive women, unloved and unwanted by anyone. We are all paid in full measure for the things we give in life. Give bitterness and unfair dealings and you will be paid in like coin. Give sincerity, love, kindness, and unselfishness, and you will be paid in that coin. Always bear this in mind when you begin to figure on getting the best of a bargain—particularly the bargain of marriage.

If you will look about, you will be sure to discover that marriages of extreme youth seldom turn out happily. The couple may remain together, but they do not harmonize. They do not get the most out of life. There is constant strife and bickering. The children do not have a fair chance to develop because the home often is a battle ground. None of the parties involved get a fair deal in this sort of marriage, so be cautious of marriage at too early an age.

When one is caught in the trap of the foolish mistake of a youngster's headstrong ideas, is it wise to forever live with that mistake and get deeper and deeper in the mire? Or is it wise to admit your mistake, wipe the slate clean, and take a fresh start in life? Even criminals are given a fresh start when they make a mistake. Surely women should be granted the privileges given criminals.

However, every woman should recognize that her happiness is not without price if she has made a mistake. When there are children, many things must be considered, for upon those who brought them into the world rests the responsibility of giving them a fair start in life.

This is a problem we face today, and one with so many angles, so many phases and circumstances, that no rule will fit all cases. It is hard to say if the children are worse off as nomads, wandering from one parent to the other, or living in a home seething with bitterness. But these are things to be considered in regard to the best thing to do for the children before divorce is begun.

At what age should a woman marry? How does she know when she has found her man? What if she marries and finds herself unhappy?

These are all questions you should ask yourself before you make the plunge. Woman can keep on searching until she finds happiness and love. Perhaps the best illustration possible as a lesson in what a woman can do with her own mind, with her life, either married or single, can be told by analyzing the Duchess of Windsor. She is decidedly the most glamorous woman of our age—and well worth studying.

Born without wealth, she struggled along in none too high style to make her debut. Soon afterward she fell in love with a young naval officer. Like all young girls who find themselves infatuated with uniforms and romance, she married. But this young lady was not content to live the rather limited life of a naval base. She found that the world was large, there were more interesting people, her mind began to develop, and she longed to grow. She realized that she had made a mistake in the selection of her husband. As fine a man as he was, he could not keep pace with the ever-growing mind she possessed. The mistake was undone in the divorce court, and they parted friends. She continued developing, learning, visiting new places, meeting new people, tasting a new and wider life. And again she fell in love—again with a uniform—and again she married. Here she had the benefit of further travel, of visiting Europe, where she began to learn new languages, new habits, new places, and to delve into the ancient background of her new home, her new friends, and her new life.

Her mind being alert, ever striving for the finest, the best, and the most select, her second husband found himself far behind his fast-developing wife. She had passed him, though they remained on the surface Mr. and Mrs., she had reached far above her humble starting point, for she had become one of an international group, familiar with many points of the globe. She found herself surrounded with the "accepted" of London, and had as her friend the man who was then

Prince of Wales. A man who had never fallen in love, a man who had traveled in many of the places she had been; a man who dared to think for himself, though he had spent his life training to be a puppet—and so their minds met.

Here is a woman who did not try to attract, but showed the capacity for a great friendship, enduring for years, before love entered. They endured sacrifice. Love once recognized as mutual, they sacrificed the world and the British Empire for that love. I hope they will always be happy.

Neither tried to cultivate personality—rather, they *grew into personalities*, which is always the acme of development.

There were younger women, more beautiful women, and women with money, youth, and beauty who were courting favor for a chance to speak to the King. But none of these could tear down the magnificence of the personality that grew and developed as Wallis Warfield's mind began to unfold over a long period of years, molded to the fineness of a Stradivarius—not even when the Prime Minister made the King choose between his throne and the personality he had learned to love.

I am no prophet. I cannot say what will be the outcome of that wedding, but after all, that is not the point that I am making. The point is that Wallis Warfield proved beyond any question of a doubt when she became the Duchess of Windsor, that youth, beauty, and fortune are not woman's greatest assets. Upon the development of a woman's personality rests her lot to remain a miserable creature, taking what Life chooses to hand over the counter, or a Queen reigning within her own little kingdom.

CHAPTER 14

How to Marry the Man You Want

By Napoleon Hill

$\mathcal{I}$ have never met the former Wallis Warfield Simpson, or the former king of England who gave up his throne to marry her, but I know enough of human nature to safely conjecture that the marriage was engineered by Wallis.

Take a look at her picture, and consider that she was a woman past forty when she married the Duke of Windsor, and you may wonder, as millions of others have, what there was about her that attracted the world's most desirable "catch" in marriage.

"That something" in the Duchess' personality, which aided her in attracting, marrying, and holding the man who gave up his crown in order to marry her, has been known to philosophers and psychologists back down through the ages. It is as old as the human race, as irresistible as the law of gravity! It is not only the attracting force with which a woman may attract and hold the husband of her choice, but it is also the power through which any person who understands its nature and use may make Life yield whatever is asked of it.

Everyone knows that Peggy Hopkins Joyce has attracted the men of her choice through a multiplicity of marriages; that she has managed always to marry a millionaire who willingly contributed to her large sums of money; but few know the secret of her success in being always able to attract a man of great wealth. She is not good-looking; she is not gifted with any form of outstanding talent; she had no advantages in the way of a family background, yet she has been able to marry men of wealth so often that no one may attribute her success to mere chance or good fortune.

Rosa Lee (Mrs. Napoleon Hill) stumbled upon this subtle force of attraction with which men and women make Life pay on their own terms, while she was in her early 'teens. I have her own father's word for it that she has always been able to get whatever she wanted, although he could not explain exactly how she managed to do it. After having lived with her for several years, I believe I am qualified to describe the secret of her strange power. Since the purpose of this book is to help other women who are earnestly seeking the Road to Happiness, I feel it both a duty and a privilege to divulge her secret.

Instead of describing the principle through which Rosa Lee has so definitely made her life to order, I will analyze the exact manner in which she has applied this principle. So no one may be unnecessarily burdened in trying to interpret my description of her system of getting what she wants, I will analyze it point by point, viz:

1. Definiteness of Purpose

From the days of her early childhood, Rosa Lee has followed the habit of knowing definitely what she wanted. Everything she has ever procured, from her first doll to her present home Castle-on-the-Hill, came to her in response to a well-defined desire for definite things. Throughout my thirty years of study of successful people, while organizing The Law of Success philosophy, it became obvious that all successful people move with this same definiteness of purpose; they know exactly what they want; that they refuse to accept defeat instead of attaining it.

So, step number one in finding and attracting the man of your choice is one you must take in your own mind, in the form of knowing exactly what type of man you demand. This question settled, you must contact the man and attract him to you; providing, of course, you have so mastered the philosophy described in this book that you have developed magnetism of both body and mind.

There are thirty qualities which go to form one's personality. Every one of them is important. You will find the entire group defined and explained in the last two chapters, and so arranged for your convenience that you can measure yourself by the list and determine exactly where you must begin in improving your personality. The most important of these thirty principles have been adequately described throughout the book.

Now let me say a few words that may be helpful to all who were attracted to this book by its title; those whose major purpose in reading the book is to attract both a man and money. When you come to the point of actually choosing a husband, be sure that he has everything you want in a husband, including money, or definite ability to earn money equivalent to the amount you want. Go over your list of "prospective husbands" very carefully, analyze each one thoroughly, and determine just how far each is capable of going in earning money. Among other things, do not fail to find out how much ambition each man possesses, for it will be much easier to convert an ambitious man into a money-maker than it will a man without this.

Before Rosa Lee agreed to marry me, she discussed with me my entire life plan. She found out what was my major purpose in life, how much money I was capable of earning, the plan through which I would earn it, and definitely committed me to a program leading to opulence. Of course she went about this in a tactful, sympathetic manner, but her purpose was to determine just how high in the scale of ambition I was capable of climbing or of being pushed with her cooperation.

Long before she ever met me—in fact, from the time when she was but a girl—Rosa Lee decided in her own mind the exact type of man she was going to marry and the monetary values he must be able to produce. From that early picture of her future husband she never wavered. When we were married, I had just lost all my money in the world depression, but that made no difference to Rosa Lee because she had already convinced herself that my earning capacity was sufficient to enable me to accumulate the fortune she desired. From the very beginning, she began to talk about living in a Castle, when as a matter of fact I was thinking more about how I was going to feed her than I was of wealth in abundance. Note well what I am saying about this, as it marks one of the most important features of getting the things you want. As I have said, she started talking about living in a Castle the day we were married and she kept right on talking about it for four years, but the nature of her talk was not that of mere nagging. Her talk consisted of enthusiastic planning of ways and means to earn the money to pay for such opulence. She organized her planning into definite periods each day. During this time she and I went away to some secluded spot, sat down, and earnestly discussed ways and means of adding to my earning capacity.

The meetings began to show satisfactory results from the very beginning. As they proceeded, we advanced from one victory to another. My literary work began to take on an entirely different, and a greatly improved style. Our very first joint literary product, *Think and Grow Rich*, was so definitely saturated with the spirit and the faith of this harmonious working plan which Rosa Lee had developed between us, that it became a best seller from the very start, and remains in that class today. If you have read that book, you will know what I mean when I say that every line of it conveys to the reader the same feeling of inspired faith we felt when we were writing it.

My purpose of relating these intimately personal details is solely that of giving you the cue as to how a woman may marry the man of her choice and, through the proper system of cooperation with him, acquire whatever money she may desire. You will observe, with benefit I hope, that Rosa Lee did not merely marry me, then sit down and wait for me to earn the money she wanted. No!—she knew, as every person of wisdom knows, that one draws from Life in exact proportion to what one puts into it. She has put into our marital relationship the encouragement, the definiteness of purpose, the enthusiasm, the concentration of effort, the imagination, and the cooperation essential to increase my earning capacity far beyond anything I had ever accomplished or ever could have done without her aid. In this way, has she put into Life an equivalent in values of that which she demands and is getting out of Life.

When Rosa Lee mentions sincerity of purpose, and advocates its development by other women, as she has done so definitely, she is confessing to one of her own habits more than she is advocating a rule of conduct for others. When she speaks of the spirit of romance, she is describing something which she practices, for it is true that she has disciplined her own mind to find and make use of the romance of every problem she encounters.

Perhaps the greatest use she makes of her philosophy is that of tightly closing the door between herself and the things she does not want from Life (such as poverty, inharmonious relationship with others, etc.) and devoting her thoughts to the romance of acquiring the things she does want. Fortunate, beyond description, is the person who has acquired the ability to do this. Fortunate is the man whose wife inspires him to close his mind against the things he does not

Fortunate is the man whose wife inspires him to close his mind against the things he does not want and to open it widely to the things he does want.

want and to open it widely to the things he does want, for he thereby removes from his mind the self-imposed limitations which condemn so many men to poverty and misery all the days of their lives.

We come now to the second point in Rosa Lee's system of attracting what she wants, viz:

2. Concentration of Effort

All successful achievement requires concentration upon definite plans for the attainment of definite ends. Remember, Rosa Lee decided at an early age the type of husband and the amount of money she wanted, but she did not stop with that decision. She gave her mind the task of carrying out her desires and kept it concentrated on that job for nearly fifteen years. She did not merely wish for a husband who would give her money; she concentrated her mind on that desire and kept it there until her efforts had been rewarded.

Psychologists are agreed that there is some strange power in the laws of Nature which tends to clothe definiteness of purpose with its material equivalent, whether the purpose be that of marrying a man and acquiring money, or some other definite objective. Rosa Lee's method of concentrating upon what she wants is simple and understandable. She begins to talk about what she wants and keeps on talking until practical ways and means of procuring it have been developed. Her father told me that all her life she has followed this habit of talking incessantly of whatever she wanted, and he admitted that as far as he had the means of knowing she had never failed to get everything she desired.

The third point in Rosa Lee's system is—

3. Poise

She has her mind under control at all times. Never have I known her to become disconcerted or to hesitate when she reached a point at which some decision was called for. I remember so well the definiteness with which she reached a decision when I asked her to marry me. I had just finished giving her a frank analysis of my financial condition from which I made it plain she would have to make temporary sacrifices on account of my strained finances. Her decision to accept me at that time meant giving up financial security she already enjoyed. It meant undertaking a job that would call for lean years and hard work on her part, but she took the step without a moment's hesitation.

In broad contrast with Rosa Lee's perfect poise, I have observed, among the thousands of women whom I have analyzed, scores of women so lacking in this quality that they literally repelled men who were interested in them matrimonially. Poise calls for self-control, which means control over both one's thoughts and deeds. Without poise, one cannot concentrate one's efforts effectively. People who become mentally "hot" and "cold," as their temperament dictates, generally find Life a disappointment. Calmness of purpose, with determination back of that purpose, are forces that cannot be permanently defeated, whether one is seeking a suitable husband or some other equally desirable form of riches.

As a part of her method of maintaining her poise, Rosa Lee has a system, or "door closing" as she calls it, through which she closes her mind tightly against every unpleasant thought that tries to enter. Once she has met with an unpleasant experience, she puts it behind a closed door and does not permit her mind to dwell upon it. Her system is so effective that it helps her to remain in perfect physical health as well as keep her mind positive at all times.

Calm determination is a state of mind every person should cultivate!

I wish I might drive home this truth so it would register indelibly in the mind of every woman who is seeking the sort of relationship in marriage that Rosa Lee and I enjoy, whether she is one who has not yet found the man of her choice or one who is married to him but still has not made the marriage bring her all that she desires. A determined man is difficult to defeat; a determined woman is infinitely more difficult to defeat. A determined man and a determined woman, working harmoniously toward a definite end, are practically impossible to defeat. I am convinced that the only thing which could defeat Rosa Lee and me would be our neglect or failure to work together in a spirit of harmony.

A determined man is difficult to defeat; a determined woman is infinitely more difficult to defeat. A determined man and a determined woman, working harmoniously toward a definite end, are practically impossible to defeat.

Another important point to watch is —

4. Drifting

A vast majority of the people of the world may be classified as "drifters." They drift in their thought-habits; they drift in their aims and ambitions; they drift in all their relationships with other people; they drift in their relationship with themselves. Drifting becomes a fixed habit. With time the habit becomes so strong that it cannot be broken.

Definiteness of plan and purpose in time become fixed habits, but with vastly different results in the lives of those who move with definiteness and determination.

I may as well here boldly state that only women who move with definiteness of plan and purpose may be sure of attracting the men of their choice and the money they desire. Attractive physical appearance, extreme beauty, refinement, education, and a pleasing personality may avail a woman but little unless she has the capacity to know exactly what she wants and forms the habit of demanding just that.

Among my acquaintanceship with women were no fewer than a thousand, many of whom were refined, educated, and good looking, yet not one of these came within sight of appealing to me as a prospective wife, although I was searching for a mate. The reason is plain. Those who wanted to marry were indefinite as to what they demanded or expected of marriage. When I met Rosa Lee, and found upon a frank discussion of marriage that she knew exactly what she expected the marriage to yield, I was drawn by some strange power which I did not then understand, to propose marriage. I now know the power that influenced me, through which both her mind and mine had been prepared to meet in a spirit of harmony which caused us to become attracted to one another as definitely as material objects are attracted by the law of gravity.

Think what you may, do whatsoever you choose, form whatever habits you please, but you cannot escape the influence of Cosmic

Habit-Force, which forces you to carry out the dominating thoughts of your mind. This law works no less definitely in attracting a man and money than it does in keeping the stars and planets in their places.

People who are successful in any calling are known to be people who develop and maintain a success consciousness. They have become "success minded" as some state it. The poverty stricken and the failures have accepted these undesirable conditions by becoming poverty conscious. That is, they have allowed their dominating thoughts to dwell upon poverty and failure. The law of Cosmic Habit-Force transforms these dominating states of mind into their physical, material and financial equivalent, using the nearest and most convenient media available for the purpose.

The mind that has been definitely charged with a clear picture of what one wants is forever on the lookout for that very thing. The mind has ingenious ways of attracting people to the physical counterpart of that which they definitely desire.

A short time ago, Rosa Lee and I dined with friends, a couple who had been married for over twenty years. The wife is a college woman and has a keen intellect, but we had noticed that she had soured on life generally; she constantly found fault with her husband, and showed signs of impatience and lack of poise in her contacts with others. We were puzzled as to the cause of her trouble until she made a statement at the dinner table, which gave us a clue as to what had happened to her. "All my life" she exclaimed, "I have sworn there were things I would not have and things I would not do. I have had to accept every one of them." With all her education and intelligence, this otherwise brilliant woman had not learned the truth that the mind attracts to one the physical counterpart of the dominating thoughts upon which it dwells. Her mistake was in thinking of and talking of that which she did not want instead of thinking and talking of that which she did want. Most people make this same mistake. The woman who fills her mind with fear, lest she will not attract a suitable man in marriage, is almost certain to see her fear fulfilled.

During the years Rosa Lee and I have lived together, I have never heard her speak of anything she did not want! But I have heard her speak constantly, and with unmistakable evidence of faith, of the things she did want. She keeps her mind so busy with thoughts of the desirable things of life that it has no time to create the undesirables. Summed up in a single sentence, her entire system of procuring from life whatever she wants may be described in these words: She decides definitely what she wants, how much of it she wants and when she wants it, then talks herself into it. Try her system and you may be surprised at the changes in your life you can bring about speedily.

If you wish to know what is the secret of most failures I will describe it as the habit of thinking and speaking of that which one does not want. The major secret of all success is the habit of thinking and speaking of the things one does want. If you want a husband and plenty of money, decide what type of man you want and how much money you desire, than saturate your mind with thoughts of these until they become the dominating influence in your mind. If you already have a husband who is satisfactory, but not as much money as you desire, begin at once to talk with him about ways and means of acquiring more. Do not nag him because he does not provide you with enough money, but inspire him with a true desire to have more. Very soon you will observe that he has picked up your enthusiasm over money and he will be more than apt to get it for you. Never speak of poverty! Never speak of anything you do not want! Do not be afraid to demand and expect

> *The major secret of all success is the habit of thinking and speaking of the things one does want.*

the best Life has to offer, for there is an abundance of everything you desire, no matter what may be the nature of your desires. Remember, your mind can acquire anything it can desire!

Before closing this chapter, I cannot refrain from hoping that everyone who reads this book will be fortunate enough to appropriate and profit by these frank statements I have made concerning the philosophy which has brought such abundant riches to Rosa Lee and me. The facts are as I have stated them. The principles we have used are exactly as I have described them. Before you spend any of your time trying to pick a flaw in anything you have read in this book, read the next chapter and take an honest inventory of yourself. Then you will be better prepared to judge the authors of this book, yourself, and every other person you know or come to know in the future.

I now turn the book back to Mrs. Hill, who contributes the remaining chapters.

CHAPTER 15

The Secret of Woman's Power over Man

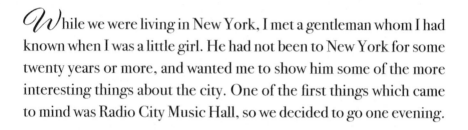

$\mathcal{W}$hile we were living in New York, I met a gentleman whom I had known when I was a little girl. He had not been to New York for some twenty years or more, and wanted me to show him some of the more interesting things about the city. One of the first things which came to mind was Radio City Music Hall, so we decided to go one evening.

Before we went, I told him that it was more wonderful to me to see the famous precision dancers than to marvel at the magnitude and beauty of the theatre itself. As you know, these dancers are world famous, and there is nothing to equal their intricate routines. As the picture ended and the lights came up for the overture, he admired the beauties of the auditorium. He marveled at the manner in which the musicians rose out of the darkness of the pit, and the effectiveness of the spectacle.

Then came the stage show. Soon the Rockettes came dancing on the stage in scanty but very beautiful costumes. They were dancing as one. Every girl a perfect match for the one next to her. Every muscle in every girl moving in exact precision with every muscle in the next girl.

We sat in silence for a few minutes, then he whispered to me, "If my wife knew I was sitting here looking at those girls with their limbs exposed, she would be disgusted." I was not certain that I had heard correctly and asked him to repeat what he had said. He made the same statement the second time.

It seems impossible to me that anyone could have such a narrow viewpoint and such a morbid mind that she could not tolerate the perfection of a dance, the beauty of a complete unit of young women trained and drilled to the perfection of the Precision Dancers of the Music Hall.

I began to think about this man and his wife. How could it be possible that the mother and father of two young girls, as they are, could be so totally unaware of the change of customs and times? I began to wonder just how they had approached the subject of Life in discussing it with their daughters. All during the rest of the show this was running through my mind, so I made the opportunity later in the evening to ask him a few questions.

The sum and substance of the manner in which they had handled the matter was this: they had completely ignored it.

I wondered if they were exceptions to the rule, or if other parents had done the same thing. I began to inquire among others who had young daughters, and to my complete astonishment I discovered that almost without exception the parents had completely avoided the subject of sex. They reasoned that any "nice" young girl will not run into any sex problems. That any "nice" young girl should not think of sex until she is married. That any "nice" young girl would not come in contact with the type of young man who would suggest sex.

How wrong are these parents! If your parents have ignored the subject of sex, and told you not to think of such things, you must consider that they are expressing a wish rather than a fact. How wrong are you, if you think you will not run into the problem of sex, and be put to it to decide just how to handle the situation. You will have to decide for yourself just what you are going to do about it, for it is a decision left entirely to the individual.

That sexual relationships among the younger people are more or less accepted as a matter of fact is recognized by all who have not closed their minds to existing circumstances. To express an opinion regarding the moral side of this is but to waste one's breath. To accept it as a fact, and deal with the circumstances is the sensible and most beneficial thing to do.

If you are unmarried, no doubt you wonder what course you ought to take.

The truth of the matter is that most of your girl friends are asking the same questions of themselves. Do not discuss this subject with other women, for women are a jealous lot. They are quick to condemn, to talk, to condemn another for something which they, themselves, have done. Remember this and keep your own counsel.

In regard to your own life, I suggest that you decide for yourself the answers to the questions which you ask. No one else can do this for you. It is a matter between you and your own conscience. It is not a matter of religion, or manmade law. Nature has no respect for the rules of human conduct as set up by human beings. She respects only her own laws, and has so deeply planted the sex urge that mankind cannot deny its existence—otherwise how did you and I get here?

No woman should ever marry any man whose main interest in her is only physical. Marriages that bring spiritual happiness and economic security are those which take place between two people who are so harmonious sexually that they may transmute their combined sex energies into whatever channels they desire, at will.

The Right and Wrong Way to Meet Men

When you first meet a man, do not take it for granted that he is in love with you and will ask you to marry him. Even though you are very magnetic and charming, if a man sees the "marrying look" in your eye, he will turn and run. This goes without exception (unless you have a mint of money), for no man wants to be trapped into marriage by a woman. Often, girls who live too much with their mothers are guilty of this too obvious marriage scheming, or their mothers are.

I know two young women who are first cousins, and they are about the same age. One of them is married and divorced. The other has never married. The divorced woman has very little sexual magnetism, but she knows how to handle men perfectly. She has plenty of dates, plenty of proposals, and lots of good times. The single woman is very magnetic, but has the most unfortunate manner in handling men.

The moment she meets a man, she assumes a possessive manner; rather resents the fact that he has known other girls, and actually presumes to deny him the privilege of going with other girls. This may be done after one has definitely committed a man to a proposal, but not before. He will give up the other girls of his own accord, if he is sufficiently interested in you.

As a result, this second young woman has remained single, and most likely will continue to do so. She has very few dates, meets very few eligible men, and is invited to few parties or gatherings, for her friends know her weakness and are not inclined to throw her at their bachelor friends.

Do not feel that age has anything to do with the art of attracting men, or the sexual magnetism of a woman. That may have been true a few years ago, but not today. Men are more interested in the sophisticated women of maturity today than they have ever been in the past. In most any community, you can find some older woman who has made a good "catch" where younger and more beautiful women have failed.

In a small town in the middle west, I met a woman who at the age of 45 met and married a young man of 28. They have been married now for some six or seven years, and they seem unusually happy. There seems to be no difference in their ages, as one would expect. He is most devoted. In fact, he is far more attentive than most men who are married to wives of their own age. This woman attracted him through her ability to understand his problems, and to hold his interest where younger women were busy in obviously trying to "make a match."

It is to be recognized as an actual fact that there is a lower side to every man. It is up to a woman to recognize this tendency, and to handle it in such a manner that it is not repulsive. She must bring his natural instincts up to her own aesthetic level, or drop down to his own level. If a woman once steps down to a man's level in anything, she immediately loses her charm and attraction for that man. I admit it is difficult to draw such a fine line of distinction, but it must be accomplished, if you are to attract and hold the man of your choice.

It is never good policy for a single woman to become involved with a married man. This goes without saying, for the odds are too great against happiness in such a relationship. It is also very unwise to mix sex and business. This is today a major problem for women who wish to succeed in the business world, for many men refuse to employ women unless special privileges are allowed. Such decisions are up to the individual and not for another to even offer an opinion. I am a firm believer in every person making decisions for herself, and not basing those decisions upon the opinions of others.

It is impossible to cut one's self entirely off from the opposite sex, or if it is done, it is such an unnatural life that the women who do it become warped and miserable in their own minds.

The young women who live in the house with older women, where there are no other young people and no men around, are apt to suffer most, for the older women have not advanced with the times. They think in terms of the conditions and customs of their own youth. Even though these women may be mothers and grandmothers, they are not confronted by or informed on the hodge-podge that has come to be our social life since the first World War.

You Must Adjust to a Changed World

There is no denying that the home, the business, professional, social, and church life of every young person is different from what it was before the war. Whether it is better or worse is entirely beside the point—it is as it is, and we must adjust ourselves to the circumstances.

If a young woman wishes to live in a world of fancy, and to dream of the romance of a gallant knight, she may do so—but she is not apt to find much happiness, for she must live alone in her dreams. The men of today are not at all like the men of yesterday, in their manner of expression. Men are men. Men have always been men. Men will always be men, and fundamentally they are just as they were in the stone age. The only difference is that we have become "civilized," and have set up certain social barriers, certain religious rules, certain laws, certain moral standards which have complicated things.

It is this changed social life which has caused so much unhappiness and unrest. The circumstances and conditions have moved faster than the minds of men and women. Perhaps it is never possible for the mature mind to recognize and admit the changed circumstances.

Perhaps it will always be that the older people will bring their children up ignorant of facts and conditions. But if that is true, it is even more true that we as young people must inform ourselves and make the necessary adjustments to fit the needs of our time. We must become a part of the world in which we live, mix with the boys and girls of our own age, the men and women who are our companions and acquaintances, and make the mental adjustments necessary to avoid being hurt or crushed by the stampede of events common in the social practices of today.

I would be the last to express an opinion on the right or wrong, the good or the bad, the progress or retreat of the social standards of the world. I feel it is too big a problem for my little mind to handle, and even if I did choose to solve the problem in my own mind, I could do nothing to correct the existing circumstances, and even less about changing the face of civilization.

Sex is one problem which must be solved by every woman for herself. It is something too intimate and too personal to even be discussed with another woman with entire frankness. It is one decision which is forced upon us by the very nature of our being, and it is the one thing which may be our greatest asset, or our greatest liability, according to how we use the magnetism and charm of our sex energy.

I cannot feel that I have done my full duty by the readers of this book without urgently requesting that those who are interested in the psychology of sex, as a means of attracting and holding the man of their choice, should read some authoritative books on this subject. A very fine book is published by the Ralston Society under the title of *Sex Magnetism*, by Edmund Shaftesbury. The Society also publishes other valuable books on this subject.

Every intelligent woman knows that her greatest lure is her feminine charms; the sexual qualities given her by Nature. But many women who are otherwise intelligent have not learned how to make the most of this attraction. In giving you my impression of the possibilities available to women through their power of sex, I am not going to preach a sermon on morals; I am not going to set up any standards to guide women as to when to use this power and when to subdue it.

There is a fine art in the proper use of the sex emotion which places in woman's hands an irresistible force with which she may influence the man of her choice to do her bidding. If I succeed in describing this art so every reader of these lines will grasp it and make it her own, I will have accomplished exactly what was intended by this intimate course of instruction.

A woman's sex emotion is something to be used as a power of attraction, through which she may acquire from Life what she asks of it. It is an asset of great or small value, according to the value she, herself, sets upon it. Sex is not only the major lure with which a woman may attract and hold the man of her choice, but it is the power with which she may attract and hold friends in every field of human relationship. Sex emotion heads the list of the 30 qualities of a Pleasing Personality.

Getting the Proposal of Marriage

At this point, I will assume that you are a single woman; that you are reading this book to gather useful information with which to attract the man of your choice. Or perchance, if you are married, that you are keenly interested in holding the man you have accepted as a mate.

Very well; let us begin our analysis by describing the manner in which a single woman may safely and effectively attract the man of her choice through uses of her sex emotion. We assume, of course, that every woman old enough to be reading a book of this nature is wise enough and experienced enough in social relationships to have attracted a number of men, among whom she has established the proper social contacts to provide her with an opportunity to make a choice among them.

Having made that decision in her own mind, a woman's next step is to influence the man of her choice to propose marriage without asking him outright to do so. This step calls for the most subtle form of sales technique. It will not permit high pressure tactics. It will not permit direct appeal. It will not stand any form of appeal which is obvious to the man. The selling must be so skillfully done that he believes he is the salesman and not the one being sold. He must be cleverly jockeyed into proposing marriage without any evidence he is being deliberately influenced. This calls for the sort of selling which only a woman can do. Women who are smartly informed on the psychology of sex understand this sales technique, but unfortunately not all women have this knowledge and skill in its use.

No matter what anyone may think or say on the subject of sex, it is woman's strongest lure and greatest asset or liability according to her understanding and use of it. As I have said, it is not the purpose of this chapter to go into the "liabilities" of sex, as these have been explained well enough in many able books on the subject. The purpose here is to point out woman's greatest asset!

If you cannot attract and hold the interest of the man of your choice through your sex magnetism, it is almost certain you cannot attract him through any other motive. Of course he may have other interests in you, but they will lack the fire of enthusiasm to make them permanent if your feminine nature does not attract him.

Able salesmanship consists in a woman's ability to discover man's most outstanding desire, plus her skill to become the means of helping him realize that desire. But some men desire other things than sex expression, such as money, fame, power in business, recognition in their professions and business callings. The woman who is truly an able salesman of herself will learn to appeal to the man of her choice by helping him attain all the objects of his desires. She will learn the art of Transmutation (see chapters three to five on that subject) and be of help to the man of her choice in helping him transform his power into worthier ends than that of mere sex expression. The women who understand how to do this are generally married to successful men, through whom they get the money and the material things of life they desire.

Remember, the emotional feeling you put into your intimate love-life is the stimulating influence that will register in your husband's mind. Also remember that this emotional feeling has more effect when it is properly expressed along the lines I have mentioned. Feeling and the expression of feeling must be combined if you wish the best results. Once you learn to express your sex emotion effectively, you will observe that you stimulate your husband and inspire him with greater imagination, self-confidence and initiative in connection with everything he undertakes.

To sum up: the woman who takes precaution against allowing her sex relationship to deteriorate into a mere physical experience is more than apt to hold her husband. Moreover, she is sure to help him in his chosen calling, and thereby help to place him in the way of providing her with all the money she needs. It is in this manner that women attract men and money! Could any other system be more practical? Could anyone find fault with any women applying her God-given power to this desirable end?

Until you have learned to be tolerant with those who do not always agree with you—until you have cultivated the habit of saying some kind word of those whom you do not admire—until you have formed the habit of looking for the good instead of the bad there is in others, you will be neither successful nor happy.

PART FOUR

*How to See Yourself
as Others See You*

CHAPTER 16

Your Personality Is Your Fortune

For Your Confidential Self-Analysis

$\mathcal{W}$e come, now, to the part of this book which calls for a personal inventory of your good and bad qualities. If you have read the book with a sincere desire to know yourself as you are, and truly wish to develop a personality which will attract whatever and whomsoever you desire in life, you will enter into this personal inventory with courage and eagerness.

After you have answered all the questions, you may profit greatly by having some person who knows you well go over them with you, to determine how well you have judged yourself on each of the qualities of a Pleasing Personality. It will be both interesting and beneficial if you will induce a number of your acquaintances to enter into the spirit of this analysis with you, each giving you her rating of you on all of the qualities. This can be done by having a number of typewritten copies made of the qualities, one to be given to each person and to be graded by her and returned to you, together with whatever comment she may wish to add concerning her estimation of your good and your less desirable qualities. To make it easy for each person to grade you frankly, the papers may be handed in to some member of the party other than yourself, and by her given to you collectively, so you will not know the author of any of the papers. If this game is played in earnest it will be most helpful to all concerned.

In a middle western city, a young woman of my acquaintance allied herself with a few other women for the purpose of deliberately developing in themselves a pleasing personality. They formed a Personality Club and limited the membership to a few who knew one another well enough to enable them to be frank in their relationship. The club met once a week, at the home of one of the members. The program consisted of a roundtable discussion of ways and means of helping each member to develop her personality. These meetings were not personal admiration gatherings; they were seriously conducted for the purpose of helping every member to know her faults and her virtues.

These young women had a definite purpose in forming the club. Each was desirous of attracting the right man in marriage. They began accumulating a library of books dealing with personal magnetism, psychology and other self-improvement subjects. By the end of the first year they had over a score of very practical books, all of which each member had read and assimilated. These books were reviewed and analyzed, one by one, during the club meetings, which is far different from merely reading them privately. Group discussion of any subject tends to clarify it.

The improvement in the personalities of these young women became so noticeable to their friends that they began to be quizzed as to the source of the improvement. This resulted in an agreement between them whereby each was permitted to invite into the club one friend.

There is room for such a club in every community. If you want a practical plan for using a portion of your time beneficially, invite a few friends and form a Personality Club. This would pay greater dividends than would membership in any bridge club or other social organization. If you are already married, you may greatly improve your marital relationship by this sort of self-analysis in conjunction with other women who are sincerely interested in improving their relationships with other people. If you are not married, you may so definitely improve your personality that you will attract the man of your choice. If you are not interested in marriage, you may so improve your personality that your relationship with others will be more pleasing. Surely no woman who is engaged in business or is holding a position in the business world will overlook the possibilities of adding to her income and her chances of advancement by improving her personality through the activity here suggested.

If you desire to enter into the organization of Personality Clubs on a commercial basis, you will find this a rich and interesting field, and this for the reason that there is a genuine need for an organized method of helping women to develop the more desirable attributes of feminine charm. To be of greatest benefit, such clubs should be conducted confidentially, and the membership should consist entirely of women who are acquainted with one another and are harmonious.

The 30 Qualities of a Pleasing Personality

1. THE SPIRIT OF ROMANCE. This is purely a state of mind which can be cultivated. It is a combination of optimism, faith, courage, enthusiasm, imagination, love, hope, and a genuine passion for self-expression through harmonious alliances with other people. A woman without the Spirit of Romance is like a flower without its perfume. The woman who has permitted the Spirit of Romance to die within her heart has closed before her all hope for happiness and much of the possibility of her helping others to find happiness. The Spirit of Romance is no respecter of age. It dwells in the hearts of the young and the old alike, if it is encouraged. It has been given the first position for definition in this list of the 30 qualities of a Pleasing Personality because it would fit nowhere else.

2. FLEXIBILITY OF PERSONALITY. The ability to mentally and physically "unbend," the habit of relaxing at will, and of becoming a part of any circumstance or situation in a spirit of harmony. Flexibility must always include the ability to sense, or to "tune in" on other people's thoughts. Also the ability to speak fluently, with poise and personal charm, with a voice control that conveys exactly the meaning intended, and the capacity to smile naturally and freely at will. Flexibility is placed near the head of the list of the principles of a Pleasing Personality because that is where it belongs. The person with a flexible personality exercises such self-control that he can quickly adapt himself to any situation in a spirit of understanding. Also, the flexible woman can cooperate with other people without friction. The flexible person can turn her enthusiasm on and off as freely as she might turn a water faucet on and off. The flexible person can become a part of her environment as easily and freely as the chameleon changes its color to harmonize with its environment. Flexibility is a quality that can be cultivated by anyone. Franklin D. Roosevelt is America's finest example of flexibility of personality. The late Calvin Coolidge was an appropriate example of lack of this quality.

3. HARMONY WITHIN ONE'S SELF. No one may enjoy a Pleasing Personality without harmony and self-control within his or her own mind. To develop harmony within, one must acquire the habit of reaching decisions promptly. Indecision and harmony are unfriendly states of mind. One or the other must dominate. Both Flexibility of Personality and Harmony depend, to a large extent, on sound physical health. A thorough cleansing of the intestinal tract often prepares the way for harmony within one's own mind. Before harmony can exist one must master the Six Basic Fears and gain control over "Old Man Worry." Communication with Infinite Intelligence is possible only to the mind in which Harmony dominates. No one can become a genius, or rise above the commonplace, snap-judgment form of thinking on any subject, unless and until he establishes complete harmony in his own mind. Every salesman worthy of the claim of ability to influence other people has the ability to establish harmony in his own mind. Plans and purposes of every nature go astray and become as nothing unless they are conceived in the mind of a person who is at peace with himself. Three of the 17 principles of the philosophy of individual achievement are essential for the establishing of harmony, viz.: The Master Mind, Self-Confidence and A Definite Chief Aim. The person who knows definitely what he wants, and has faith in his ability to get what he wants, and is associated with others in a spirit of harmony for the purpose of attaining a definite goal, seldom is defeated except temporarily.

4. EFFECTIVE SHOWMANSHIP. To become an able showman, one must develop a keen sense of dramatic values. Nearly all circumstances and facts in life are commonplace and uninteresting until they are embellished by some form of drama. To dramatize situations, facts, and realities, they must be so organized and presented as to capture the imagination of people. Effective Showmanship is largely a practical method of influencing people through their imagination. Most stage plays would be without interest if separated from the necessary stage equipment and appropriate costumes. Imagine actors trying to play Romeo and Juliet in a bare room, with Juliet standing on a bare table, dressed in a plain house dress. The successful salesman of merchandise is successful because of his ability to inject into his sales presentation sufficient showmanship to grip the imagination of the prospective buyer. Master Salesmen generally sell ideas as well as merchandise. The merchandise is incidental. The important thing is to paint a dramatic, colorful, pleasing picture of the usage of the merchandise. The publisher of the *Law of Success* sold 1,000 sets of these textbooks to one buyer, but he did not describe the mere printed pages of the books. What he actually sold was the LIFE TIME EXPERIENCE OF ANDREW CARNEGIE, HENRY FORD, THOMAS A. EDISON, JOHN WANAMAKER, JAMES J. HILL, WOODROW WILSON and more than 500 others of equal prominence—the actual experience that was written on the pages of the books in language that anyone can understand. Being an able salesman, and knowing the value of Effective Showmanship, the publisher of these books did not try to sell the paper and printer's ink of which they consist, worth at most a few dollars. Instead, he sold the organized, tested and tried lifetime experience of more than 500 of America's best known and most successful men, worth a king's ransom to any person seeking definite knowledge on the subject of personal success. (NOTE: *The Law of Success* philosophy mentioned above is an eight-volume set of books by Napoleon Hill, and published by the same concern that gets out the book you are now reading.)

5. THE MAGNETIC HAND-SHAKE. Conveyance of personal magnetism, through the popular custom of hand-shaking, indicates enthusiasm or lack of it. Moreover, this custom definitely indicates flexibility of personality or lack of it. "Charming" people convey friendliness through the shaking of hands. Of course they must feel friendly before they can convey that feeling. "Personal magnetism" is sex energy under another name. Highly sexed people generally are known to be "charming" but not everyone knows the source of this personal charm. Magnetism must exist before it can be passed on through the handshake. But there is an art in the method of doing this. The hand must be gripped firmly but it should never be squeezed until the one being thus greeted writhes in pain. The hand is a perfect barometer through which a person experienced in such matters may determine how much or how little personal magnetism one possesses. Perfection in hand-shaking grows out of careful study and practice.

6. APPROPRIATENESS OF CLOTHING. First impressions are lasting. The clothes may not "make the woman" but certainly they go a very long way toward giving her a favorable introduction. Clothing not only makes an impression on others, but it MAKES ALSO AN IMPRESSION ON THE WEARER! Clothing is an important part of one's media through which effective showmanship may be used. There is a law of Nature through which "like attracts like," and this law operates in favor of the person who is appropriately adorned, by attracting to that person those who are prosperous and self-reliant. Fresh, clean clothing of appropriate design, according to one's occupation, gives one self-reliance and flexibility of personality. An unshaved face and a soiled shirt give the feeling of inferiority to the ablest of men, and every woman knows that appropriate clothing is nine-tenths of what people call "beauty." The dress-maker's bill and the beauty parlor bill of the "charming" woman may be staggering in amount, but these two items often are her greatest asset, no matter what her physical appearance may be.

7. POSTURE AND CARRIAGE OF THE BODY. Alertness in posture and carriage of the body definitely indicates alertness of the brain. Character analysts of ability wish to see their clients when in motion, while walking or at play. Brisk steps and quick, rhythmical movements of the body indicate quickness and harmony of thought. Stooped shoulders, shuffling movement in walking, and slouching position while sitting all indicate menial slovenliness. Correct body posture is the result of training and habit. It not only gives one a favorable appearance, but it also tends to give one sound health. Flexibility in movement, quickness of step, high chin, square shoulders, all are a part of correct body posture which help to give one a Pleasing Personality.

8. CONTROL OF VOICE. The tone, volume, pitch and "coloring" or feeling mixed with one's voice, are important factors of a Pleasing Personality. Because he knows how to control his voice, Franklin D. Roosevelt has been called "the man with the million dollar radio voice." Harsh, nasal tones should be eliminated. High pitched, tenor voices should be toned down for conversational purposes. Guttural and rasping tones should be controlled. Pleasing tones of voice are released from the roof of the mouth and not from the throat and chest. The most pleasing sentence ever uttered by a human being is said to be "I LOVE YOU MY DEAR." The pleasing part of the sentence is not found in the words but in the FEELING in which they may be spoken. Whether one realizes this truth or not, most people subconsciously judge others by the tone of their voices more than by the words they speak. This is notoriously true of women. It is doubtful if there lives a woman so dull in the interpretation of the meaning of words as not to know when a man speaks truth or falsehood when he utters that five word sentence, "I love you my dear." The convincing lawyer, preacher, salesman, politician, or business man is the one who deliberately and with purpose aforethought, injects FEELING into his spoken words, coloring his words so they cannot miss conveying the exact meaning intended. There are no less than a hundred different ways of saying "I love you my dear." Only one of them carries weight and CONVINCES. Last, but not least, REMEMBER THAT YOUR

The pleasing part of the sentence is not found in the words but in the FEELING in which they may be spoken.

WORDS ALWAYS CONVEY DEFINITE MEANING SEPARATE AND APART FROM THEIR GRAMMATICAL MEANING, AND THEY MAY, THROUGH YOUR CARELESSNESS OR NEGLECT TO GIVE THEM THE MEANING YOU WISH THEM TO CONVEY, ACTUALLY DO YOU GREAT INJUSTICE. The purpose of words is to convey ideas and impulses of thought from one mind to other minds. The "coloring," emotion, feeling you put into your words, AND NOT THE WORDS THEMSELVES, often determine how other people interpret your meaning. Facial expression is one way by which words may be and generally are given "coloring." Even an experienced actor cannot successfully express words that do not harmonize with his feelings without disclosing this fact through the expression of his eyes and face.

9. SINCERITY OF PURPOSE. This quality requires but little explanation. Obviously, lack of sincerity of purpose will be fatal to the development of a Pleasing Personality, for the reason that this deficiency reflects itself in the tone and quality of one's voice, and in one's facial expression. A philosopher expressed this truth impressively when he said, "What you are within your own heart speaks to me so plainly that I cannot hear your words." Sincerity of purpose gives one poise, self-reliance, faith, courage, perseverance, and colors every word one speaks, and writes itself indelibly in one's facial expression. Lack of sincerity of purpose DOES EXACTLY THE SAME THING.

10. CHOICE OF WORDS. Words are the chief media for the conveyance of thought. They should harmonize with the thought one wishes to convey. Slang, colloquialisms, profanity, and mispronounced words may pass, but they never can gain for one a favorable impression. So-called "wise-cracks" may go on the moving picture screen, but they will serve no good purpose for the man or the woman whose major purpose in life is to get somewhere and be somebody. Being "smart" through the use of trick words is one thing. Being impressive through gentleness of thought and correctness of speech is something else. The person aiming to acquire a Pleasing Personality will be contented to let others use the "smart" words. Boys and girls of the high school and college age are the worst offenders in the use of "wise-cracks." Be not alarmed over their destiny. Like the measles and the chicken-pox, this tendency to play upon words runs its course and eliminates itself by its own dead weight. Let us not be prudish. There are times, of course, when slang and a bit of polite "wise-cracking" serve to lighten the occasion and break down formalities so people will be at ease. The trick is in knowing when and where to indulge this form of levity without carrying it over into the daily habits of speech. Let us all remember, lastly, that every time we open our mouth and utter a word we are confessing to all who hear us, the quality and nature of our character and thoughts. Let us be careful what we confess. Let us remember, also, that "smartness" of expression among friends and acquaintances who know us is one thing, while such expression in the presence of strangers, or those of short acquaintance, is something entirely different. Whether we realize it or not, those whom we meet for the first time have us always "on the spot." That which comes out of our mouths is construed to have originated in our heads, and that which we say is "used against us," while newly made acquaintances are getting our mental, spiritual and professional range through our own expression of words. Speak no words in the presence of a stranger or a newly made acquaintance unless you are willing to have your moral status and your intellect judged by your words. You judge other people by

Every time we open our mouth and utter a word we are confessing to all who hear us, the quality and nature of our character and thoughts.

what they say in your presence and by their personal appearance. They judge you in the same way.

11. POISE. This quality, so essential for a Pleasing Personality, is largely the outgrowth of self-reliance, definiteness of purpose, self-control and appropriate personal adornment.

Sound health plays a part, too. Poise begins with harmony within one's self. Indecision and poise make poor bed-fellows. Fear, worry, anxiety, greed, vanity, and egotism are fatal to the development of poise.

12. A KEEN SENSE OF HUMOR. Without this quality, there can be no adequate expression of flexibility of personality. This quality generally is inborn, although it can be cultivated. Its development begins by acquiring the habit of refusing to take people, and life itself, too seriously. People who fall into the mistake of trying to be "dignified" usually do so because they are taking themselves too seriously. Too much dignity is fatal to keenness of humor. The habit of hearty laughter, even though it must be a forced, artificial habit, will soon cure exaggeration of dignity.

13. UNSELFISHNESS. Unselfishness attracts people. Selfishness repels them. One of the queer traits of selfishness is the fact that it makes itself known to everyone except the person who is giving it housing. Selfishness is the twin-sister of greed. Discovery and elimination of this unsavory trait of human nature usually must be the work of the experienced character analyst. When the individual looks for selfishness in himself, he usually misses it because he looks through biased eyes that are literally steeped in selfishness. Moreover, he does not expect to find it and tries hard not to disappoint himself. A dangerous trait of human nature is this habit of measuring other people through standards created by ourselves. The author of *The Law of Success* once earned $1,000.00 by the simple process of permitting a man to take a look at himself through the author's eyes. What the man saw caused him to detect and to correct a trait of character which had already cost him a fortune. Thousands of people paid that same author $25.00 each for a similar privilege and not one of them failed to express gratitude for the discoveries they made. The most dangerous trait of selfishness is its ability to hide from the person who gives it shelter and suffers by its presence. Do not be too sure you are free from this evasive enemy just because your best friends have not told you of its presence. If the advertisements may be relied upon, "your best friend will not tell you if your breath is offensive." You would not believe him if he did, because you cannot detect the evil odor and therefore assume it does not exist.

14. FACIAL EXPRESSION. The dominating thoughts of one's mind reveal themselves through the lines of the face and the expression of the eyes. A "hard" face means a "hard soul." Worry, fear and anxiety cause the corners of the mouth to droop. Courage, optimism, hope, and definiteness of purpose cause the corners of the mouth to curve upward in an expression of softness. Pain causes one to contort the muscles of the face into disagreeable expressions. Negative, disagreeable thoughts have the same effect, but they shape the lines of the face more slowly and subtly, and also more permanently. A sharp pain in the stomach will make one resemble a clown. Silent thoughts of greed and dishonesty and avarice and revenge and hatred make one take on the appearance of a thief, or a criminal. If your face has elements of hard expression, stand before a mirror and practice until you learn how to soften the expression. Meanwhile, find out what caused the "hardness" and begin correcting that from within, through your thoughts.

15. POSITIVE THOUGHTS. Negative thoughts and Pleasing Personalities are never found together. Positive thoughts are those associated with courage, self-reliance, faith and definiteness of purpose. Thoughts which cause one to look to the future and not to the past. Thoughts which see in every tomorrow a new and an unborn opportunity to be seized and made the most of, no matter what has happened today or in the past. Thoughts which build but never destroy. Thoughts which see in every failure the seed of an equivalent success. Thoughts which have no time to devote to ways and means of "getting even" with enemies or striking back at those who have offended.

Negative thoughts and Pleasing Personalities are never found together.

16. ENTHUSIASM. This trait of personality is the chief medium by which feeling and "coloring" may be added to one's spoken words. There are two forms of enthusiasm. One is active and the other is passive. Stated differently, one is expressed through words or actions while the other is expressed only through FEELING. Each is appropriate on occasion. Sometimes, enthusiasm that is felt but not openly expressed through either words or deeds is the more effective of the two, for it is true that the brain is a broadcasting station through which one's thoughts may be passed to the brains of others. Passive enthusiasm is beneficial in two ways. It may give power to one's silent thoughts and it may give character to one's facial expression. It must be remembered that enthusiasm, without self-control, may be very dangerous. It may lead one to give out expressions of thought where silence would have served better. Enthusiasm has wings that travel rapidly, and because of this truth, no one can have a secret, not even in his own thoughts, without control over enthusiasm. Thoughts that have been blended with enthusiasm pass from one mind to other minds with the rapidity of light, unless they are controlled.

17. SOUND HEALTH. Auto-intoxication, indigestion, bad teeth, a hardened liver, and a Pleasing Personality do not get along well together. Find out what causes these conditions and correct them. Many women are not very pleasing during the menstrual period because they do not give this physical condition the proper attention. Modern medical science has prepared a remedy for this objectionable condition. The fear of Ill Health is one of the six Basic Fears any one of which may destroy a Pleasing Personality. This fear generally is cultivated by people whose minds dwell upon ill health until they develop a disease known among physicians as "hypochondria" (imaginary illness). A hypochondriac is not a pleasing person. Remember this when you begin to describe your operations or start to tell others you "enjoy poor health." Sound Health usually is the outgrowth of a sound, positive mind that is so busily engaged in carrying out some DEFINITE MAJOR PURPOSE in life that it has no time for sickness.

18. IMAGINATION. Alertness of the imaginative faculty is one of the more important factors of a Pleasing Personality, because it is the faculty through which one may dramatize words and ideas so they become more impressive. It is the faculty which gives form and direction and purpose to the impulses of thought. It is the faculty that receives problems and creates ways and means of solving them. It is the faculty that gives brilliancy to conversation. It translates the dull and the common-place events of life into intense and highly colored affairs which grip and hold one's interest. It enables one to create new ideas by combining old ideas in a new arrangement. Truly, the imagination is the workshop of the soul wherein may be fashioned the plans and purposes which control one's earthly destiny. The imagination becomes keen and alert through USE.

19. TACTFULNESS. This quality needs but little if any explanation. It assumes great value as one of the factors of a Pleasing Personality because it serves as a censor over one's words and deeds, seeing to it at all times that no word is spoken and no act is indulged in that may offend others unnecessarily. Sometimes, this quality enforces silence where silence is best. At other times, it commands speech, but suggests what one should say and when one should stop.

20. VERSATILITY. Perfection in this quality makes it necessary for one to know where and how to acquire any desired knowledge on short notice, and to possess full and complete knowledge in connection with one's occupation or calling. (See lesson one, on the Master Mind, in *The Law of Success* for detailed instructions on ways and means of acquiring and using the knowledge of other people.) The quality of versatility may be made to assume its full value as one of the factors of a Pleasing Personality by all who understand and apply the principle of the Master Mind.

21. THE CAPACITY TO BE AN ATTENTIVE LISTENER. It is more profitable to be an attentive listener than it is to be an able speaker, and this for the reason that the attentive listener not only pleases those to whom he shows this courtesy, but he also places himself in the way of acquiring their entire stock of knowledge, and of profiting by their experience. The worst of all "bores" is the person who habitually follows the practice of cutting in and taking the conversation away from others before they have finished speaking. Observe those who make this mistake and be convinced.

It is more profitable to be an attentive listener than it is to be an able speaker.

22. ABILITY TO SPEAK EFFECTIVELY IN PUBLIC. Perhaps no other quality of a Pleasing Personality may be made to lift one as high as that of the ability to speak convincingly in public. It is the one factor through which one may place one's self in the way of opportunity. It is an advertising medium second to none and one that costs nothing except the effort essential to obtain perfection. In politics, in most of the professions, in religion, and in practically every form of business, the ability to speak forcefully is priceless. It is the one dependable tool by which the individual may gain attention and lift himself to leadership in his calling. Perfection is attained only by painstaking, persevering endeavor. Effective speaking cannot be taught. ONE MUST LEARN IT. The rules must be created by each individual for himself. Fine gestures, correct speech, proper wearing apparel all help, BUT THEY DO NOT MAKE EFFECTIVE SPEAKERS. The most impressive speeches are impromptu. They come from the heart and not from the head. Studied lines and memorized sentences may sound beautiful but they never can equal the spontaneous outburst that is motivated by SOME STRONG DESIRE OF THE SPEAKER. To speak well one must FEEL DEEPLY, and one must know much about the subject of one's speech.

23. PERSONAL MAGNETISM. This quality is known, under another name, as sex energy. It is biological in nature and the quantity possessed and used by an individual can be increased through the proper exercises. Deep down within you, woven into the very fiber of your being, lies this vital attracting energy. But it will sleep forever unless you arouse it. Do not overlook the cultivation of personal magnetism. (See the *Law of Success* textbooks for a full description of the nature of personal magnetism and how it may be transmuted into financial and business and professional success.)

24. GOOD SPORTSMANSHIP. Everyone admires a clean sportsman. Everyone admires the quality of sportsmanship which prompts one to be a good loser when misfortune overtakes him or her. Good sportsmanship assumes that one can win without boasting and lose without squealing.

25. PROMPTNESS OF DECISION. The habit of reaching decisions quickly and of reversing them slowly, if at all, assumes proportions of great importance as one of the factors of a Pleasing Personality with all who are engaged in any form of leadership and all who aspire to leadership.

26. COURTESY. No other single quality pays as high dividends as that of plain, everyday courtesy, no matter what may be one's calling. A full and complete statement of the values of courtesy, and of ways and means of gaining these values, will be found in the lesson on THE HABIT OF DOING MORE THAN PAID FOR, in *The Law of Success*.

27. ABILITY TO SAY "NO" PLEASINGLY. Some people are so unfortunate as to make enemies of those whose requests they have to refuse. The ability to say "no" without offending is an art that calls for careful cultivation, but the reward is worth the effort.

28. THE BEAUTY PARLOR HABIT. No woman can appear pleasing to others if she neglects her skin, hair, nails, and facial lines. This sort of service should become a regular habit. Moreover, the service should be supplied by a beautician who has the artistic ability to make the service fit the physical requirements of the patron; a beautician who is, in reality, a Personality Artist. Best results can be had by patronizing the same beautician regularly instead of shopping around. The Beauty Parlor Habit may be costly, but it will pay dividends in personal appearance and in monetary outlay.

29. HABIT OF SMILING. Franklin D. Roosevelt has what might be called a million-dollar smile. His smile is pleasing because it is natural and comes from the heart. It is not a studied, or a stage smile, of the variety for which the late Theodore Roosevelt was so famous. A pleasing smile disarms one's adversaries, aids digestion, adds to one's courage, and helps in a thousand other ways to gain for one favorable advantages.

30. HABIT OF BEING DEMOCRATIC. Aloofness, snobbery, and haughtiness have cost men and women heavily. The truly great always have been and always will be democratic, plain, and approachable by all who have any right to claim their attention. Ornate office furnishings, "private" doors, and personal secretaries serve a necessary purpose, but sometimes they serve too well by depriving those who hide behind them of genuine opportunities to benefit by freedom of contact with less formal people. President Franklin D. Roosevelt hit a trip-hammer blow of strategy when he first entered office, by communicating directly with the people of America, over the radio stations. The greatest leaders in business and industry are those whose office doors are wide open at all times to the most humble workman. Democracy inspires confidence and builds friendships which endure for life. Snobbery and formality close the doors that lead to friendship.

———

These 30 factors are not all the qualities of a Pleasing Personality, but they are the ones of greatest importance. Fortunate is the person whose personal analysis discloses a 100 percent grading on all of these factors.

To know yourself as you are, you should measure yourself step by step, using the 30 factors of a Pleasing Personality as a measuring stick. This experiment will bring you face to face with yourself, disclosing to you traits and faults which you may have overlooked previously. To get the most out of this self-analysis, put yourself on the defensive and deliberately look for weaknesses.

You cannot avoid making some kind of impression on the people you meet. Whether you make a good impression or a poor one is a question you should be able to answer. Every word you utter, every expression of your face, every move you make, every thought you release, the clothes you wear, and the people with whom you associate most closely, all serve as markers by which other people get their impressions of you. Through these media, you are selling yourself, for better or for worse, whether you are conscious of this fact or not. You can see, then, the importance of KNOWING DEFINITELY what sort of a personality you actually have, for your personality is the medium by which you are rated in every contact you have with others and every opinion they form of you.

---

*The charms of a virtuous woman make her
an agreeable companion for her husband;
the charms and graces of woman lose
not their influence like beauty.*

CHAPTER 17

How to Make an Accurate Self-Analysis of Your Personality

*D*o you ever have an opportunity to take a look at yourself through the eyes of other people? Do you know definitely what others think and say about you when you are not present, and why they judge you as they do? Has it ever occurred to you to ask yourself why some people rise to great heights of personal success with but little schooling? Have you ever wondered how Henry Ford bridged the wide chasm between poverty and a huge fortune, or how Thomas A. Edison became the world's most successful inventor, despite the fact he was sent home from school after three months of attendance with a note from his teacher informing his parents that he had an "addled" mind, and did not have enough sense to take an education?

Have you ever seriously asked yourself why you have not risen as high on the ladder of personal achievement as your intelligence and schooling and ambition entitle you to rise? Perhaps all these and other questions may be answered when you shall have answered the questions in the Personality Test Chart, for here is presented a completely organized description of the more important factors through which successful men and women in all walks of life lift themselves to affluence and power.

People who achieve success do so because of their ability to sell themselves to other people in a favorable light that gains for them the cooperation of others. The factors of successful personal sales-manship are 30 in number. They are the 30 principles of a Pleasing Personality. All of these 30 principles can be developed by anyone who wishes to get ahead in the world.

Give Yourself an Accurate Check-Up on Your Rating on the 30 Qualities of a Pleasing Personality

IMPORTANT NOTICE: Rate yourself, in the space provided for that purpose at right hand side of page, opposite each of the 30 qual-ities of a Pleasing Personality. The ratings are "Good," "Fair," and "Poor." Give yourself the "good" rating only when you feel you are entitled to 100% rating.

If you rate yourself fairly, you may easily bring to your attention some characteristic, mannerism or trait which has been standing between you and the position in life to which you aspire. It will give you an accu-rate inventory of the facts concerning yourself of greatest importance to you in the business of selling your way through life successfully.

The "Good, Fair, and Poor" ratings are just for each of the 30 Qualities. The individual questions for each quality call for "Yes," "No," or otherwise appropriate answers.

1. Flexibility of Personality   G | F | P
(ability to adapt yourself to all sorts of situations without irritation or embarrassment)

Are you at ease, or embarrassed, in the presence of others?

Do you become confused, or "rattled" in emergencies?

_____

Have you control over your temper at all times?

_____

Do you converse freely with others, or do you permit others to lead you in conversation?

_____

Have you complete control over your affections?

_____

Are you liked best by men or women?

_____

Which do you like best, men or women?

_____

Do uninteresting people "bore" you, and if so, do you show it?

_____

2. Harmony within Self   G | F | P

(sufficient self-control to master your feelings and to overcome all forms of fear and worry)

Are you at peace with yourself, in your own mind?

_____

What annoys you most frequently?

_____

What do you fear most?

_____

Place an X by the following six basic fears by which you are most disturbed:

Poverty _____

Ill Health _____

Criticism by Others _____

Loss of Love of Someone _____

Old Age _____

Death _____

What is your worst habit?

_____

3. Effective Showmanship   G | F | P

(ability to dramatize the commonplace events of life, to give life and color and action to words, thoughts, and deeds, so as to attract favorable attention from others)

In your personal dress, are you known as a smart, medium, or poor dresser?

_____

Have you had experience in public speaking?

_____

Do you make a bid for attention in a gathering?

_____

Do you understand and practice the subtleties of suggestion in your speech and personal habits?

_____

Can you lead men, in a conversation, into the discussion of any subject you desire, or away from any subject desired?

_____

4. The Magnetic Handshake   G | F | P
(ability to shake hands pleasingly)

Are your hands soft?

_____

Hard? Warm? Cold? Large? Small?

_____

Fingers long or medium?

_____

Do you endeavor to impart "feeling" when shaking hands?

_____

Are men attracted to your hands when you shake hands?

_____

Do you respond with a gentle or firm grasp when you shake hands?

_____

How often do you have your nails manicured?

_____

Do you use bright-colored or deep-colored nail polish?

_____

5. Appropriateness of Clothing   G | F | P

Do you select clothing of colors and patterns best suited to
your physical type?

_____

Do you like evening clothes or street clothes best?

_____

Do you match in color your clothes, hats, shoes, pocketbook, etc.?

_____

Describe your underwear.

_____

6. Posture and Carriage of Body   G | F | P

Do you stand erectly?

_____

Shoulders back or stooped?

_____

Do you step briskly or slowly in walking?

_____

Are you graceful in movement?

_____

Do you sit erectly, or slouch in your seat?

_____

7. Tone Control of Voice   G | F | P

Is the pitch of your voice high, low, or medium?

_____

Do you sing? Have you had voice training?

_____

Can you put feeling and expression in your voice?

_____

Do you depend upon the tone of your voice to emphasize words?

_____

8. Sincerity of Purpose   G | F | P

Do you retort to subterfuge, or are you open and direct, by nature?

_____

Do people take you into their confidence freely?

_____

Whom do you trust most, men or women?

_____

Do others trust you?

_____

9. Choice of Words   G | F | P

Do you use slang in conversation?

_____

Have you the habit of "wise-cracking" in conversation?

_____

Do you use profanity?

_____

Tell risqué stories?

_____

Are people attracted to you when you speak, or do they show indifference?

_____

10. Poise   G | F | P
(mental and physical self-control)

Are you nervous, and do you show it?

_____

Do you have self-confidence at all times?

_____

Do you worry, and if so, about what?

_____

Do you express your likes and dislikes freely?

_____

11. Keen Sense of Humor   G | F | P

Do you laugh freely and heartily?

_____

Are you considered "stilted" or "high-brow"?

_____

Can you take a joke on yourself without offense?

_____

Are you democratic, dignified, or reticent?

_____

12. Unselfishness   G | F | P

Do you think of yourself first on all occasions?

_____

Do you willingly render useful service to others?

_____

Do you grant favors as freely as you ask them of others?

_____

13. Facial Expression   G | F | P

Do you scowl or frown at times?

_____

Are the lines of your face "soft," "hard," or "medium"?

_____

Do you smile when you speak?

_____

Do you indicate your state of mind by your facial expression,
or have you what is known as a "poker face"?

_____

14. Positive Thought   G | F | P

Are you of a suspicious nature?

_____

Are you optimistic or pessimistic by nature?

_____

Do you "nag" or find fault with relatives?

_____

On which class of thoughts does your mind dwell most, those associated with fear, or those associated with faith and courage?

_____

15. Enthusiasm   G | F | P

Do you speak with enthusiasm?

_____

Over what do you become enthusiastic most quickly?

_____

Do you always express the enthusiasm as you feel it, or do you hold it in check?

_____

16. Sound Health   G | F | P

Is your health good, fair, or poor?

_____

What physical ailment, if any, have you?

_____

With what form of illness do you suffer most often?

_____

Do you ever become ill from worry?

_____

Do you become nervous during menstruation?

_____

17. Imagination   G | F | P

Do you control your imagination, or does it control you?

_____

Do you write, or have you ever desired to write?

_____

Do you plan a task before you begin it?

_____

Have you thought of taking up a profession, or occupation,
and if so, what?

_____

Did you ever put an old idea to new use, and if so, what was it?

_____

18. Tactfulness   G | F | P

Do you always express your thoughts freely?

_____

Under what conditions do you lack tactfulness?

_____

Are you more tactful with men or women?

_____

Do you try to influence people through persuasion, or how?

_____

19. Versatility   G | F | P

On what subjects are you best informed?

_____

What are your personal accomplishments?

_____

Have you business ability, and if so, what sort?

_____

What are some of the books you have recently read?

_____

20. Capacity to Be an Attentive Listener   G | F | P

Do you "break in" and take away the conversation when another person is talking?

_____

Can you listen without showing signs of being "bored" when another person is speaking?

_____

21. Ability to Speak Effectively in Public   G | F | P

What experience have you had in public speaking?

_____

On what subjects would you prefer to speak in public?

_____

Would you like to be an able public speaker?

_____

22. Personal Magnetism   G | F | P

(sex emotion)

Are your sex desires rated as high, low, or medium?

_____

What relationship, if any, do you see between sex emotion and a pleasing personality?

_____

Do you know how to transmute (transform) sex desire into some other form of effort, at will?

_____

Have you ever experienced what you would call a truly great love?

_____

Have you been disappointed in love, and if so, with what after-effects on yourself?

_____

Can a woman love more than once?

_____

What is your conception of the difference between sex emotion and love emotion?

_____

Do you believe that clothes, cosmetics, perfumes, and dainty lingerie may be appropriately used to enhance one's sex appeal to the opposite sex?

_____

Do you believe it is a "sin" for a woman to make herself alluring by careful attention to clothes and body adornment?

_____

What do you believe a man seeks first in the choice of a wife?

_____

23. Good Sportsmanship   G | F | P

Are you considered a good loser?

_____

Would you cheat in a friendly game of cards?

_____

Would you cheat in the game of love?

_____

Do you always give to others the same privileges you ask
for yourself?

_____

Would you speak disparagingly of one of whom you
were jealous?

_____

What is the best rule by which a woman may hold the man of
her choice?

_____

24. Promptness of Decision   G | F | P

Do you reach decisions slowly or quickly?

_____

Do you reverse your decisions quickly or slowly?

_____

In connection with what do you procrastinate most often?

_____

25. Courtesy   G | F | P

To which are you most courteous, men or women?

_____

Are you always courteous to servants, waiters, and salespeople?

_____

Are you courteous when driving an automobile?

_____

Are you impatient when someone seems to neglect you?

_____

26. Ability to Say "No" Pleasingly   G | F | P

When it is necessary for you to say "no," do you make friends
or enemies usually?

_____

In what terms do you refuse a beggar who approaches you?

_____

27. The Beauty Parlor Habit   G | F | P

Do you patronize a beautician regularly?

_____

What service do you procure?

_____

What cosmetics do you keep on hand?

_____

28. The Habit of Smiling   G | F | P

Do you smile freely at all times?

_____

Can you cover the effect of embarrassment with a smile?

_____

Have you ever forced yourself to smile when you felt like crying?

_____

When you were mad?

_____

Have you ever compared the lines of your face when smiling with those when you are frowning?

_____

29. The Spirit of Romance   G | F | P

Do you have a romantic nature?

_____

Have you ever been compelled to suppress the spirit of romance?

_____

30. The Habit of Being Democratic   G | F | P

Are you inclined to hold yourself aloof from others?

_____

Do you show by your manner that you think yourself better
than others?

_____

What traits in people do you dislike most?

_____

Definition of a Pleasing Personality

The sum total of 30 qualities developed and blended in habits of
dress, speech, posture, and mental attitude and mannerisms which
give one a dominating position in business, social, and professional
relationships with others.

A PLEASING PERSONALITY goes much deeper than mere
outside, physical embellishments. Good looks, a perfect figure, a
soft skin, proper grooming, and color harmony in dress all add to
one's physical charm, but to be truly pleasing to others one must
have personal charm that comes only from within, by development of
the 30 qualities described in this Personality Test-Chart.

If you have already answered the questions you have observed, of course, that you know infinitely more about yourself than you knew before you began to answer the questions.

The information upon which this system of personality analysis was developed was gathered over a period of more than 25 years through scientific research and accurate analysis of more than 25,000 people. The system is searching, definite, and accurate. It discloses both the weak and the strong points. The purpose back of the analysis is that of correcting faults and helping one to discover and make use of one's greatest assets.

The great highroad of human welfare lies along
the old highway of steadfast well-doing; and they
who are the most persistent, and work in the
truest spirit, will invariably be the most successful;
success treads on the heels of every right effort.

Afterword

Good Bye and Good Luck

And so we come to the end of our journey together in learning HOW TO ATTRACT MEN AND MONEY. So long as life lasts, women will seek to attract men—for it is the inescapable law of Nature.

Do not think that a one-time hurried reading of the book is all there is to it. It is distinctly something that has to be studied and earnestly applied. Each time you return to these pages, you will develop more of the technique—and uncover more of the power—to gain the treasures of life which you seek.

Study the many chapters with an earnest resolution to make the most of them, and nothing can stop you from winning whatever success within human bounds you may desire. It is all up to you. Never permit yourself for a single moment to become discouraged. Opportunities often come forth from the most unexpected places.

May the teachings of this book build in you a supreme confidence, for you will have mastered a philosophy written by one who has proved it is sound, and who has made it work.

It is the author's hope that HOW TO ATTRACT MEN AND MONEY will carry you to—and keep you in—that happy harbor for which every normal woman was created—the wife of the right man.

THE HILLS AND THEIR HOBBIES

ROSA LEE HILL'S hobby is children. She has begun to help homeless children who have no opportunity to get a fair start in life. It is an educational experiment aiming to teach them how to become self-respecting, self-reliant citizens—based upon her husband's Success-Philosophy.

Already the first child has undergone such dramatic changes in character and personality that Mrs. Hill is working on definite and scientific methods by which boys and girls throughout the United States may have the same advantages.

To provide a fitting home for this experiment—in what the Kansas City "STAR", in a feature article headed "TO REAR THE PERFECT FAMILY"—the Hills have acquired a beautiful estate in Florida, illustrated on other side of this page.

A prominent real estate dealer, in a special article in the Mount Dora newspaper, is quoted:

"I had the rare privilege of helping transfer title of one of Florida's most unique estates to one of America's most distinguished author-philosophers. - - Having entertained Mr. and Mrs. Hill in my home and having had the privilege of close contact with them, I am prepared to say that both of them possess a rare fortune of a nature which cannot be measured in money or material things.

"Castle-on-the-Hill, where their work will be carried on, is a perfect setting for this 'Model American Home' where these children are to be taught. I am not overstating the facts when I say that the nation at large and the State of Florida in particular are to be greatly enriched by this unusual experiment."

In a letter to her publishers, and referring to the book "HOW TO ATTRACT MEN AND MONEY", the author wrote:

"This book is the sort that could not have been written until it had first been lived. I waited until I was almost thirty years of age before I found either my husband or our Castle, and when I did find them, *I did so by applying the philosophy I have presented in this book.* In short, I HAVE PROVEN MY PLAN WORKS!"

The following pages present a "true confession" from two married people who have made married life a Paradise of happiness. The authors hope the book will do as much for you.

CASTLE-ON-THE-HILL; Overlooking Lake Dora, Florida.

Residence and Literary Work-Shop of
Mr. and Mrs. Napoleon Hill.

Views of parts of this famous showplace.

In this Castle, set in the midst of beautifully landscaped grounds, and commanding a far-reaching view of silvery Lake Dora—the Hills are doing many things to lighten the burden of thousands of people. They are helping others to make Life pay, as it is paying them, on terms of their own making.

They are writing books for men and women; books in which they are frankly describing the methods that have brought them love, riches, happiness in abundance, and the respect of their fellow men all over the world. Some of their books are briefly mentioned on the first page of this volume.

HOW TO
ATTRACT MEN
AND MONEY

An intimate revelation for Women past eighteen.
With some facts Men ought to know—especially
those who wish to stage a come-back after ex-
periencing defeat.

*   *   *   *

A New Philosophy of Proven Methods that
will help single women find and marry the
right man—will guide married people to
marital happiness—and enable all wom-
en to inspire the men of their choice to
achieve greater financial success

*   *

By ROSA LEE HILL

With special contributions by her husband—NAPOLEON HILL
—Author of "THINK AND GROW RICH"; "HOW TO
SELL YOUR WAY THROUGH LIFE"; "The LAW OF
SUCCESS Philosophy" etc.

1940
Published by THE RALSTON SOCIETY, Meriden, Conn.

Printed in Great Britain
by Amazon

83452480R00139